Untold Tales From The Bush Leagues

By Rick Schultz

More Books by Rick Schultz on Amazon.com, Audible.com and iTunes. Choose from Kindle, paperback or audio versions:

A Renegade Championship Summer: A Broadcaster's View of a Magical Minor League Baseball Season

Come along for the ride with the 1999 New York-Penn League Champion Hudson Valley Renegades. Hear from the players and coaches who made it happen, including superstar Josh Hamilton and many other household names!

101 Things I Wish I Knew Before I Bought My First Home: How to Reduce the Stress of Your First Purchase

Buying your first home is sure to be one of the most exciting, yet stressful times in your life. This book will fill you in BEFOREHAND about some of the many issues you may encounter when you buy your home. Reduce the stress and enjoy this special time in your life!

101 Things I Wish I Knew Before I Sold My First Home: How to Sell Quickly with Less Stress

Selling your first home is sure to be one of the most exciting times in your life. This book will fill you in BEFOREHAND about some of the many issues you may encounter when you sell your home. Sell your home quickly, with less stress, so you can enjoy this special time in your life!

Rick Schultz is the Sports Director at WFUV Radio, Fordham University. For decades, WFUV in New York City has provided the training and preparation for countless nationally-acclaimed sports broadcasters and media professionals.

Contact him at:
SportscastersClub.com

For The Schultz Girls –
Jackie, Tessa and Emma

Preface

I was fortunate to broadcast my first professional baseball game in 1994. Now, more than 20 years later, I am often asked what minor league baseball life is like. Is it exciting to ride on the team bus? Do you get to go into the dugout? What are the players like? Most often, my answer is that minor league baseball is a traveling freak show circus. (I heard a player once call it that…and it fits!)

The beauty of baseball – especially in the minor leagues – is that you never know what you'll see. Most of the time, the bush leagues seem as far from the glitz and glamour of the big leagues as you can imagine, and each day seems to bring a new story or memory that one could never have imagined. The best part - each one is usually more unusual than the last! I vividly recall driving home from the ballpark each night, amazed at the people I'd met or things that had transpired during that day at the park.

Over my years in minor league baseball, I've been fortunate enough to witness many of these zany and comical things firsthand. In fact, I still cannot believe some of the unbelievable tales I've seen with my own eyes. I've traveled to many ballparks, met countless interesting people, and built up a wealth of wacky minor league memories. Still, I'm just one broadcaster. I've only experienced a small sliver of the tales that could be told.

As I began thinking about some of the most unusual things I've seen in minor league baseball – and how I could share these stories with you - I also wondered what other broadcasters have seen. The minors are home to so many talented broadcasters, many of whom will never go on to call games in sold-out, major league ballparks. These are the guys with stories to tell. Some have been calling games for 10, 20 or 30 years. They've spent hours on the bus, hung out in dugouts, eaten lousy ballpark food and called inning after inning all across the country. They have some unbelievable stories to tell, and this book will share some of their tales.

What follows in this book is a collection of some of the most bizarre, unusual and funny baseball stories as told by some of the great guys in the game. Each of these 21 broadcasters volunteered their time and talent to share, in their voice and style, some of the unbelievable things they've seen in minor league baseball. They eagerly joined this project in the hope that you, the reader, will have the most accurate picture of the unpredictable minor league world.

These are some truly great professionals from around the country. If one of these guys is calling game in your town, consider yourself lucky. They each had a great deal to bring to this project and without them this book would not exist. I owe them all a great deal of thanks – for their time, generosity, effort and some of the most amazing stories I've ever heard!

To answer the questions above – Yes, it is very exciting to ride on the team bus….until your legs cramp up, you have to use the potty or the bus breaks down on the side of the road. And yes, the dugout is a great place to learn and see a lot of interesting things. As for minor league baseball players, they are a unique bunch that does some crazy things. I hope this book allows you to witness some of those things firsthand, as if you were there. I hope these stories – from broadcasters across the nation – give you the true feeling for what minor league baseball is all about.

The broadcasters in this book are some of the most knowledgeable, talented and listened-to in the country. Thankfully, these great broadcasters have taken the time to share their wonderful memories with us all. After reading these untold stories, you will have a true feeling of what minor league baseball is like. I hope you enjoy them.

- Rick Schultz, Summer 2016

Oncoming Train

WHACK! The team was startled awake as the bus came to an abrupt halt. It was almost 3 a.m., and the ball club was driving somewhere in New York State after a late-night contest in central New York. "What the heck was that?" I thought. "What is going on?"

Trying to open their eyes in a sleepy daze, players' heads began to pop up. To the right I saw a bright, solitary light. As the light grew larger, I could place the loud, familiar rumble. Then we heard even louder honks from a deep horn. Our team bus was on a train crossing, and the WHACK had been the train crossing arm coming down right on the bus, approximately over the third aisle of seats.

"What the heck are you doing!" yelled a player from the back. "Back the bus up!" The driver, seeming oblivious to the panicked cries from the passengers, didn't make a move.

By now, we were all awake and most were probably wondering, "Is this it?" The train came hurtling toward us, and the screams from throughout the bus got louder.

WOOSH! The train whizzed past the front of the bus, no more than ten feet away. We let out a collective sigh, as the final cars of the train zipped by.

"When I woke up and saw the light coming right at me, I thought it was all over," said the manager, who sat in the front seat. The bus driver, still seeming unconcerned with the entire event, lurched the bus forward and continued to drive.

With a sly look on his face, he glanced back toward the passengers.

"I knew I had it all the time," he said.

-Rick Schultz

Season With Air Jordan

I had the pleasure and honor of broadcasting Michael Jordan's only professional baseball season in 1994. The whole season was a story and some of it was told during the ESPN documentary, "Jordan Rides the Bus".

I have plenty of stories but my favorite was the day we played basketball…In August of 1994, the Barons played a Sunday day game…After many of our day games, our team would play basketball on a local outdoor asphalt court. In fact it was the court where many of the players stayed.

Michael drives up that day, after weeks of pleading for him to play. We wind up playing a 3 on 3 and I happen to be on his team. The ball comes to Michael and I do what you are supposed to do-set a pick. He looked down on me (after I set the pick) and said, "CB, I don't need that" then he stepped backed and swished a long jumper. I didn't realize until later, that I actually had a pair of the original red/black Air Jordan's on.

At the end of the game, Michael rubbed my wife's stomach as she was pregnant with our first child. About a week later, my daughter, Chloe was born.

End of Story,

-Curt Bloom

Binoculars

Every self-respecting member of a press box has a pair. Binoculars are an integral part of a broadcaster's equipment. Some guys have huge binoculars that help you count how many hairs are sticking out of the pitcher's nose. Others use a tiny pair that only a person with eyes the size of lemonheads can use. I just need a steady pair that doesn't give me a raging headache when trying to see who's warming up in the bullpen.

Binoculars are great for peering into the dugouts, watching meetings on the pitchers' mound and getting in on arguments. They help broadcasters get a little closer to the game. The real reason, however, that every person in the press box has a pair of binoculars is to get a little closer to the crowd. To put it mildly…we're checking out the fans.

I don't feel that I'm letting anybody in on some press box secret. Anyone that looks up from the stands can see us watching everyone during the inning breaks. And fans are doing the same thing during the game. The media just have a better vantage point in the press box.

Ballparks are incredible places for people watching. With a few thousand people at a minor league game, some mighty interesting people are hanging around. That's why some fans who don't like baseball go to the ballpark in the first place. They're checking everybody out.

On Tattoo Night in Little Rock in 2001, I saw a leather-clad man leading his heavily tattooed girlfriend by a leash attached to her neck. While chaining her to a fence to get a beer, he caught me gawking at the ridiculous scene. His freakish eyes stared directly into my binoculars and I quickly turned away so not to set him off.

But even my quick exchange with Captain Caveman could not have readied me for the afternoon of August 19, 2001. That Sunday afternoon the Travs played their final regular season home game against the Midland RockHounds under a perfect blue and sunny sky.

After the top of second inning I pulled my binoculars to my eyes and scoured the stands. I stopped at the 15th row of section F in the first-base box seats and saw a petite, dark-haired girl in her early 20s. She sat with a friend, talking and smiling thoroughly enjoying the ballgame and the summer heat. My binoculars stayed pinned on her. I was mesmerized and she was beautiful. She featured a gorgeous smile and freckles galore. The way she walked told me that she was a sassy lady.

All of a sudden, she looked directly at the press box and caught me staring at her. She flashed that amazing smile and tilted her head. Although I felt like a fool at the time, I smiled back and waved at her. For that split second I forgot where I was.

Then I realized that the commercial break was over and went back to calling the game. I tried not to pay her much attention for the next two innings, but my curiosity got the best of me after the fourth and I locked in on her. She caught me again, but this time she waved at me. I lowered my binoculars, stunned for a split second, I waved back. Then she raised her right hand and put up three fingers. Then one finger followed by two fingers. I wondered what she was doing.

Did the scoreboard have the count wrong? Was she telling me how old she was? Then it hit me and I almost fell out of Ray Winder Field's open-air press box. This gorgeous, young lady was giving me her phone number from 100 feet away! Hurriedly I scribbled it down on my scorebook and then got back to the game. I was too shocked to respond to her.

For the rest of the game we exchanged glances and smiles. Finally, after what seemed like an eternity, the final out was recorded and the fans got up to leave. If not for my post-game show I would have leaped down to the seats. She left the ballpark without saying a word and I was left to my post-game show.

We had two days off before heading to West Texas for a 12-game road trip that would end the season. One day before heading out on the trip, I sat in my press box and gathered the courage to call her. I dialed the number…and it was wrong. WHAT?!?! I wrote down the wrong phone number? Out of all the stupid things that I had done…wrecking the car when I was 16; staying out until 2 a.m. the night before the SAT exam…this was the worst. There was nothing I could do. I didn't know her name and I didn't know where she lived or worked. I screwed up big-time!

The next day I hopped on a plane and flew to El Paso to start the road trip resigned to the fact that I would never see that gorgeous baseball fan again. I was wrong.

Thankfully the Travs made the playoffs due to a first-half East Divison Championship. We began the first round in Little Rock against the Wichita Wranglers on September 2nd. Gametime was 7:30 p.m. and she got to Ray Winder Field at 7:00 p.m. That's ten minutes before the pre-game show started. Perfect timing!

From the press box, I saw her and bolted to the grandstand. She stood in the souvenir line and I walked right up to her. I extended my right hand and asked her name.

"I'm Julie," she told me. "And why didn't you call me?"

I fessed up to the idiocy of my writing the wrong number and got her real phone number. We talked one hour after the Travs beat Wichita. We talked the next night right before the Travs headed out to Wichita to finish the series. I learned that she had just moved to Little Rock from St. Louis, her hometown. She was here to work for a major retailer's corporate office.

I spent eight long days on the road in Wichita and Round Rock, including September 11 in the Hilton Garden Inn. Julie and I spoke on the phone every day. And when the Travs Luxury Liner returned to Little Rock, I went home, showered, shaved and drove to her apartment for our first date.

We've had about eight hundred dates since then…and we were married on December 6, 2005 right across from Busch Stadium in downtown St. Louis.

I loved baseball from as far back as I can remember. It seems perfect that I would find my true love at the ballpark.

I still have binoculars in the press box and I always will. But these days, I only use them to look into the bullpen and dugout. Honestly!

-Phil Elson

Postgame Trade

Most radio broadcasts in minor league baseball follow much the same format as any radio broadcast you'll hear for your local major league team. A typical night on the air will consist of a pregame show, actual game broadcast, and postgame show. The postgame usually consists of a scoring recap, interview and perhaps a look ahead to tomorrow's game. One really unique thing about minor league baseball is that teams often pipe the radio feed into the home clubhouse, where they can hear the entire broadcast, especially the post-game show.

Late one season while broadcasting for a pretty mediocre club, my broadcast partner, Bill Rogan, masterminded a fun idea. The players on the club often commented that they listened to our postgame show on a boom box in the clubhouse while showering up after the game. Not that we could ever pull it off, but Bill envisioned how great it would be to somehow create a "fake" postgame show.

As the season progressed and the team fell further out of the playoff hunt, we passed the time by honing our idea. We didn't want to just do it…we wanted to do it right and make it a most memorable postgame extravaganza. Late in the season, we decided to try to put our plan into motion.First, we created a script for out "fake" postgame show, in which one of the team's players would get traded to another organization.

We specifically chose one of the more hot-headed players on the team, as to increase the chances we would get a memorable reaction. Boy, were we right. This player was a good guy, and one we thought would find the whole thing funny after the fact.

Next we collaborated with the team clubhouse manager, who would assist in our duplicitous postgame show. We would create the "fake" postgame show, and the clubbie said he'd slip the tape into the boom box and play it in the clubhouse, as if it were the real, live radio broadcast. He said he was up for the task and that nobody would even notice.

Finally we ran the idea past the team's manager and coaching staff, in an effort not to cause any major, unwanted disruption of the team's normal routine. (When high-paid prospects are involved, we didn't want to take any chances) After hearing what player we chose to be the subject of our "fake" trade during the "fake" postgame show, they were more than happy to give us their blessing.

On the chosen day, we covertly slipped our taped, "fake" postgame show to the clubhouse manager, and our plan was a go. He snuck the tape into the boom box during the game, and it was all ready to go when the team entered the clubhouse after the contest. When we went to our first "real", live commercial break, he hit "play" and the "fake" postgame show began, only for the team in the clubhouse.

As the team undressed, our "fake" postgame show resumed. We came back from our commercial break and immediately said we had important breaking news regarding the team. We stated seriously that there had just been a trade and it involved a member of the team. We acted the script out perfectly, as if we were just getting the information from the wire that minute. We named the player and how shocked we were that he was traded.

Now, as this "fake" postgame show played, the clubhouse grew silent. The players were in stunned disbelief, including the player we had "traded". As we went through details of the trade on air, we became increasingly critical of the specific player.

"Well, it's probably a good thing they traded him," I said. "He's been pretty bad all year."

"That's right," Bill echoed. "He's really been lousy and the team won't miss him at all. His control is so bad he couldn't hit the broad side of a barn."

"Definitely true, Bill," I countered. "This is a classic case of addition by subtraction.

"A BIG addition," Bill responded. "This is a win for the ballclub to get rid of this guy."

As our comments became more pointed and humorous, the player in question really began to steam in the clubhouse. He was downright fuming, and became more irate with each verbal jab. Finally he had enough. He picked up a weight ball and fired it across the clubhouse! The five-pound ball of lead just missed the team's biggest and most highly paid prospect! Immediately the manager, coaches and some players jumped in and grabbed him, telling him it was a joke.

When we arrived in the clubhouse following our "real" live postgame show, the player was sitting in the manager's office on the couch, surrounded by the coaches and clubhouse manager. They were all imploring him to calm down, telling him it was all an act and that he wasn't really traded. They even produced the audio cassette from the boom box to prove it was all a joke. When we entered the manager's office, the exasperated player looked at us and burst into a huge, confused smile.

"Good one," he said. The "fake" postgame show had worked beautifully, without a hitch. This was one postgame show none of us would ever forget.

While leaving the clubhouse, we walked past one of the team's veteran pitchers. Thanks, we said, referring to the help he gave in restraining the incensed player.

"No," he said with a sly grin, "Thank you!"

-Rick Schultz

The Kid

I have so many great memories of my time spent broadcasting in the minor leagues. However, my most fond and heartfelt experience didn't entirely come on-the-air.

It was July 30, 2002 at Dodd Stadium in Norwich, Connecticut before the Norwich Navigators (Yankees AA team) and Binghamton Mets (Mets AA team) game. I was the co-emcee of a pre-game home run hitting contest between Dave Winfield, George Brett, Mike Schmidt, Carlton Fisk, Johnny Bench and Gary Carter. The event was completely sold out. Over 8,000 fans were packed into this small, New England ballpark.

It was my last year broadcasting professional baseball. I had spent seven years in the minor leagues and had decided just weeks before that I would move on to something else after the season ended. So, the opportunity to be a part of this was going to offer a memory of a lifetime.

Now, as a baseball fan, I was pumped to meet these legends. They were some of the best players to ever play the game. These guys were All-Stars, World Series heroes and all Hall of Famers. And while each of them was great to interview and fun to interact with, I was really only interested in meeting one…Gary Carter. I grew up in Yorktown Heights, New York as a die-hard fan of the New York Mets. As a kid, baseball, and the Mets, was my life. My position on the field was catcher and my icon was "The Kid", Number 8, Gary Carter. I had his posters on my door, autographed pictures on my wall and his jersey hanging in my closet. Gary Carter was my guy.

In 1985, Gary's first season with the Mets, he hit a walk-off home run to beat the Cardinals on Opening Day at Shea. The sellout crowd chanted Gary-Gary-Gary…and I was there. In 1986, when the Mets came back to win one of the most memorable World Series in history, I went to Game 1 and was glued to the television for the next six. And from 1990-91, when Gary moved on to the Giants and Dodgers, I stayed up far past midnight just to watch him catch.

For each team that Carter played for, my Dad bought me his jersey. I was in 5th grade when he was traded to the Mets and in high school when he retired with the Expos. Needless to say, as I got older, the jerseys got smaller! I didn't realize how "cozy" they became until the night of July 30.

Despite working in professional baseball for seven years at that point, I never met Gary. In my position, I was very fortunate to meet some great players in the game…but they weren't Gary. Even in my house in Norwich, 10 years after Carter stopped playing, I had his pictures on my wall and book on my desk. For 17 years, all I really wanted from baseball was to meet my boyhood idol.

Finally, on a beautiful mid-summer night, the day had come. Before the event, all of the Hall of Famers met with the Navigators players in their clubhouse. I, too, was there and got a chance to introduce myself to them. My interaction with Carter was brief…a quick hello, handshake and a smile. It was a simple exchange.

I waited most of my life for that moment and was appreciate to have it. But, unlike many other fans who finally get the chance to meet their favorite player for just a heartbeat, I knew I was heading down to the field to spend the next hour with mine.

The six legends were split into two teams – American and National. Winfield, Brett and Fisk were on the American team and the first base side – where they were introduced and interviewed each round by a local TV anchor. Schmidt, Bench and Carter were on the third base side – where I introduced and interviewed them. Like any home run hitting challenge, contestants from both teams would advance after each round. In this case, the two finalists would go to the plate four times.

The contest began with the American team leading off. After a few home runs to get the crowd warmed up, it was the National team's turn at-bat and for me to introduce Gary Carter. Knowing for weeks that I would get this opportunity as co-emcee, I knew that I had to do something unique for the fans and of course, Carter. So, I wore Gary's four jerseys, one on top of the other and hiding each in every layer, with a Navigators jersey over them all.

As Gary approached the plate for the first time, and while I introduced his name, I unbuttoned the Navigators jersey to reveal his Montreal Expos uniform. He, and the crowd, laughed.

As luck would have it, Gary hit enough homers to advance to the next round. It was time for me to introduce him again, and just like a few moments earlier, I unbuttoned the Expos jersey to reveal his Los Angeles Dodgers uniform. The crowd and Gary got a kick out of that as well.

Carter moved on to the semifinals, allowing me to yet again remove a jersey. As he stepped up to the plate, I peeled off the Dodgers jersey to flaunt his San Francisco Giants uniform. At this point, I think the crowd got the idea…and my act may have been getting a little tired. Even Johnny Bench was over it, hopping out of his seat to grab my mic and ask me what else I had under there.

Finally, two legends reached the finals…and one was Gary Carter. He was matched up against Dave Winfield. Gary was to hit first, and of course, be introduced once more. With the audience anticipating another jersey, I gave them what they expected…but with a twist.

This time, I stopped Carter on his way to home plate and said "Kid, I grew up during your hey-day with the Mets and '86. I was in 5th grade when I got this one…so it doesn't fit as well as it used to." At that moment, I pulled the Giants jersey over my head to proudly display a skin-tight, painted-on New York Mets jersey with Carter's name and number on the back. This shirt stopped at my mid-section…literally. I was 11 years old when I got it. I was 5'5 then.

That night, I was 26 years old and 6'4. Needless to say, it was a snug fit. The crowd erupted in laughter. Gary threw down his bat and turned his head to the sky with a huge smile on his face. He walked over and gave me a big handshake and hug. Gary pulled me forward and said "Man, that was awesome."

It was one of the coolest moments of my life.

Gary went on to lose in the finals on a home run hit by Winfield in his final swing. After the event, I asked Gary if he would join me on the radio for a half inning. He agreed and met me in the press box in the third. For three outs, in a crowed booth filled with reporters, friends and family, Gary and I talked baseball, his days with the Mets and the unforgettable childhood memories he provided me.

When the interview was over, Gary signed anything and everything I had collected over the years, including the Expos jersey, his book and a framed picture. He even gave me and signed the batting glove and hat he wore in the event.

It was one of the most special nights of my life…and it happened in the minor leagues.

-Mark Leinweaver

And I now pronounce you....

Radio play-by-play is all about painting the word picture. As the announcer, you have a great seat and you want to put the listener right there next to you so they can see the game. That usually involves the description of a high, towering, home run or a leaping catch to save a run.

One night in Lowell, Massachusetts was a little different. The team I was working for, the Pittsfield Mets, was in town to play the Lowell Spinners, an affiliate of the Boston Red Sox. Someone from the Spinners apparently thought it would be a good promotion for two fans to get married at the ballpark ... during the game! I guess if they did it before or after the game, nobody would be in the stands.

So there we are, in the middle of a professional baseball game, when time is called for a wedding to be performed right near second base. The problem we were having on the radio is we didn't have enough commercials to fill the time until the game would resume. We brought on a few guests to talk baseball, but the wedding still wasn't over. What did we do?

We did the only thing we knew how to do: play-by-play. The bride, wearing a long white dress, turns to her left and leans in to kiss her new husband. I often think of that now in cable news when describing some strange breaking news event. Just tell the people what you see.

On that night, we saw a wedding .... at a baseball stadium.

-Connell McShane

Missing The Alarm

While broadcasting for Shreveport of the Texas League, Doug
Greenwald found out how costly a little extra sleep can be. When
the team had an early bus trip the morning after a night game,
Greenwald would routinely stay up all night to ensure he'd arrive in
plenty of time for the bus. Then, as the bus embarked on its trip,
he'd nod off for some sleep in his seat.

One night during the 2000 season, the team had a rainout prior to a 6
a.m. bus departure to Round Rock, Texas the next day. Since the
game was postponed, he arrived home much earlier than usual and
decided to change it up and get some sleep before the early-morning
bus. Looking forward to a little extra rest, Greenwald dozed off. He
woke up at 6:38 a.m. for the 6:00 a.m. bus.

In a full sprint out of bed and to the car, Greenwald knew he had
missed the bus and, as a result, would have to drive himself on the
road trip. He headed to the ballpark to pick up the radio equipment;
however it wasn't in its usual spot. Someone had loaded it onto the
bus, even though Greenwald hadn't made it in time. Confident that
his headphones and mixer were safe with the team, he headed out
Highway 79, the one route from Shreveport to Round Rock.
Greenwald pulled into the hotel at 1:00 pm, shortly after the team
had arrived. When he entered the hotel lobby, most of the players
were milling around, just hanging out. The irony was that *their*
rooms weren't ready for them to check in yet, although the late-
arriving Greenwald was able to check in and go to *his* room.
Following the stop in Round Rock, the team travelled on to San
Antonio, with Greenwald following the bus in his car. The getaway
game in San Antonio went 15 innings, and team was unable to
depart San Antonio until 12:00 midnight. They began the 7 hour
drive back home to Shreveport, again with Greenwald driving
himself. The entourage arrived back home at 7:30 a.m. Luckily for
Doug, they had reached the All-Star break and now had 3 days off to
rest. Greenwald arrived home, deposited his luggage, turned the air
conditioner on, took a long shower and slept all day. He never
missed the alarm again.

-Doug Greenwald

Josh Hamilton's Southern Delicacy

2010 American League MVP Josh Hamilton began his professional career in 1999. Late that summer he was called up to the New York Penn League, to join the minor league Hudson Valley Renegades in their quest for the league title. The 18-year old Hamilton had been the first overall pick in that year's amateur draft, and by some accounts was one of the best prospects ever.

As Hamilton took his initial round of batting practice that day, you could feel the anticipation in the stadium. Ushers stopped cleaning seats and peeked up to catch a glimpse of a star in the making. With great fluidity, Hamilton drove the ball in all directions. Even with the great first round of B.P., Hamilton later admitted to having some jitters hitting in front of his new teammates for the first time.

"I was like 'Just hit the ball, just hit the ball,'" Hamilton said after the round.

Before Hamilton's first game that day, team clubhouse manager Matt Veronesi shared his "Tidbit of the Day", a daily feature of the radio broadcast which filled fans in on obscure team facts they otherwise wouldn't have known. He reported that Hamilton had a right, as per his contract, to take any uniform number he wanted. His favorite number was 22, but another player already had that number. Hamilton said no big deal and took number 30. Classy move by the 18-year-old.

The team was in a tight situation a couple weeks later, needing a win on the final day of the season to clinch a spot in the playoffs. That afternoon, Hamilton sat in a comfortable clubhouse recliner and chomped on his favorite – a banana-mayonnaise sandwich.

"This is great," he said, reaching for his third sandwich. "You mean you've never tried it? It's a southern thing."

"That is disgusting," said Veronesi, working nearby. "I can't believe you actually *eat* that!"

"Oh, come on. It's good." Hamilton answered with a smile.

"I'll tell you what," Veronesi said, "If you guys make the playoffs I'll eat a banana-mayonnaise sandwich, and Rick can broadcast it on the radio. How's that?"

"OK, it's a deal," Hamilton said.

The Renegades then went out and won 7-1, clinching the wild card and a spot in the playoffs.

Two days later, before Game One of the wild card playoff series, clubhouse manager Matt Veronesi sunk his teeth into a thick banana-mayonnaise sandwich.

"It's not too bad," he said with his mouth full. "It's ok. It's not something I'd go home and make myself, but it's not that bad after all. It's edible." His face was grimaced, and he wasn't too convincing with his opinion of the sandwich. "Anybody else want the rest?" he asked. "Really, it's good, just have some."

It took Matt about 15 minutes to finish the sandwich, and I bet he hasn't had another one in two decades since.

-Rick Schultz

Record-Setting Playoff Game

In 2010, I was fortunate to witness the first Midwest League Championship Series the city of Clinton has seen since 1993. After two grueling three-game playoff series and a tough game-one loss to the Lake County Captains, the LumberKings were looking to get even in game two of the best-of-five series, their final action in front of a home crowd that year.

Things looked great for the Kings early as skinny shortstop Gabriel Noriega lined a two-run single as part of a three-run fourth inning. Clinton held a 6-2 lead heading into the seventh inning, but the Captains tied the score in the ninth on a two-run homer by leadoff-hitting Delvi Cid.

The LumberKings had a chance to take the victory in the bottom of the ninth after a one-out double by Mickey Wiswall and an intentional walk, but Captains reliever Jose Flores would strike out two batters to strand the runners and send the game to extra innings.

An already epic seesaw battle grew in legend as we passed through the 10th and 11th innings with no changes in score. The Captains then scored the go-ahead run to make it 7-6 in the top of the 12th as Roberto Perez lifted a 3-2 pitch to the left-field berm for a solo homer. The Kings would answer back yet again, however, thanks to an infielder who had played a total of one regular-season game with the club.

Carlos Ramirez stood at the plate with two on and two outs and was down to his last strike facing Owen Dew. He'd come through with the biggest clutch hit of the entire postseason, lining a game-tying single past second-baseman Kyle Smith to score Tim Morris. Mario Martinez was also waved home for the potential game-winning run by manager John Tamargo, but a perfect one-hop throw from right-fielder Greg Folgia had him out at the plate.

We went on into the 13th inning. LumberKings' reliever Jonathan Arias struck out the side, and James Jones started the bottom half with a single to left. A sacrifice bunt, intentional walk, groundout and lineout followed, keeping the game tied.

There was no change in the 7-7 score through the 14th and 15th innings, despite a leadoff baserunner for the Captains in the top half of the 15th. The same story occurred for Lake County in the 16th, when their leadoff man was stranded after a sacrifice bunt, fielder's choice and a flyout.

The 17th inning saw left-handed starter Nick Czyz come on in relief for the pitching-strapped LumberKings. He'd work past a leadoff single as well, getting help from his catcher Blake Ochoa to catch Smith stealing, and would then issue a strikeout and induce a groundout to end the inning.

Finally in the home half of the 18th, fatigue took its toll. Captains' lefty Giovani Soto, also pressed into emergency relief duty despite being scheduled to start the very next game, issued two-out walks to Ochoa and Morris. Martinez, the man who had been thrown out at the plate in the 12th to keep the game going, hit a hot smash right at third-baseman Adam Abraham. The ball ate him up, going between his legs. Ochoa rounded third and scored, sending the 100 or so remaining fans – and myself in the press box – leaping in jubilation.

The longest-ever Midwest League playoff game ended on Abraham's error, officially five hours and 37 minutes after the first pitch. Thankfully, the next day was a travel day for both teams as the knotted Championship Series shifted to Eastlake, OH. Both teams, and my voice, deserved the rest.

-Dave Lezotte

Drive Thru

After most night games, minor league players don't leave the ballpark until at least 10:30 p.m., once they have a chance to shower and dress. This is when they finally have a chance to eat a late dinner.

When playing on the road, finding decent culinary choices at that hour is usually quite daunting. As glamorous as professional baseball can be at times, these are times when players are forced to choose from some very slim pickings.

One night at about 11:00 p.m., following a game in Staten Island, New York, the Hudson Valley team bus pulled to the side of the road and we were given 30 minutes to find some food and get back to the bus. On one side of the street was a dingy convenience store.

A ways down the road was a fast-food joint, which nobody could tell was open for sure. Most of the team took the sure thing and headed for the convenience store. The place was open – that much they knew with certainty. Just two pitchers and I decided to see if we could land some hot, fast food at the place down the street.

After a five-minute walk, we arrived at the door of the restaurant only to find it locked. However, the sign said "drive thru open all night." So we did the only reasonable thing we could do, and we circled around the building to the drive thru. We stepped up to the illuminated menu and tapped on the speaker.

"I'm sorry sir, we can't serve you," said the voice from the small metal box.

"What do you mean," we moaned.

"I'm sorry, I can't serve anyone without a car," he replied defiantly.

"But we don't have a car. All we have is a bus," one of us yelled. "The drive thru is the only thing open!"

"Can't help you. Goodbye," the voice said curtly. As we slowly walked away, muttering curses to each other, an employee emerged from the front entrance.

"Listen guys, that stinks. I feel bad for you," she said. "Let me take your order and I'll go in and get it." Kindly, she did.

It took some luck, but we dined on juicy burgers and hot fries that night while the rest of the team had to manage with candy and chips.

-Rick Schultz

Practical Joker

Baseball is famous for its practical jokers and one of the best we've had in Salt Lake was one particular relief pitcher. Unfortunately for this pitcher, one his best pranks was an expensive one for him.

The team was in Vancouver and he waited for a couple of his teammates to leave their room. After the coast was clear, he somehow was able to get into it and proceeded to remove the sheets and blanket from one of the beds. He then took the mattress off of the bed and took it into the shower where he completely soaked it. After he was done, he put the mattress back on the box springs and then made the bed as neatly as the maid that worked in the hotel.

A while later, the two teammates made it back to their room for a mid-day nap. Well, when one of them laid down he went "squish". He sank down into the cold wet mattress and become soaked as well.

This pitcher had a great laugh until the hotel sent him a bill for $400 to replace the ruined bedding.

-Steve Klauke

Taxi Taxi

It was a picture perfect late morning in New England on Sunday August 21st 2003. The Norwich Navigators, who I was the radio voice for, were wrapping up a 3 game set at Hadlock Field against the Portland Seadogs. It's customary in many levels of baseball for the road team to arrive on a bus in two waves for a game. The trainer, guys who may need batting practice, players nursing an injury, etc, usually arrive earlier than the starting pitcher, some of the regulars, or guys who simply don't want to be at the park too early.

The game was scheduled for high noon and the Doubletree where we were staying wasn't too far away from the hotel. On most days many of the players would simply walk to the park but since it was a getaway day many of the players got on the first bus with their luggage. In this instance I had a friend of mine named Sam who had driven up to take in a couple of games that weekend. He agreed to drop me off at the Stadium around 1030am. As we were leaving a bunch of the players were waiting for the second bus and I thought nothing of it. As I get to the ballpark I notice that the bus was parked towards the back of the lot and blocked by a couple of cars. The bus couldn't get out of the lot. My first thought was how are the guys back at the hotel going to get here?

I popped my head into the mangers' office, briefed him on the situation and he wasn't too happy about this. I told him I had an idea and since the bus wasn't going anywhere he was certainly open to it. I had Sam head back to the hotel and pick up the remaining players…and their luggage! He was more than happy to do it as we called one of the players to let them know what their new mode of transportation would be. Since I had a broadcast to prepare for I went up to my booth but I was able to see one of the two trips that he made bring some of the Navigators to the Park. It was quite a spectacle to see ballplayers jumping out of a car and dragging their luggage less than hour before gametime!! The pregame craziness wasn't a factor as Norwich won that contest 7-5.

-Brett Quintyne

All About The Benjamins

Most minor league organizations are filled, at least in part, with former players who just can't stay away from the game. Some manage, some coach, some work in the front office and others travel as roving team instructors. It is always a thrill to meet former players, and soak up some of their knowledge, experience and perspective. After profitable big league careers, many of these former players stay involved solely for the love of the game.

Quite a few stories come to mind when I think about some of the financial conversations I've heard in the minor leagues. I can recall one former star from the 90's being involved in a heated conversation with members of the team. They were discussing all the crazy things they would hypothetically do for a million dollars. Those stories are for another kind of book.

In another financial conversation with a former major leaguer, we asked how it felt to be set for life. "Real, real good," he said. Money didn't come up often, but when it did it was often quite memorable.

I remember a summer day in the mid-90's, when an instructor was in town to work with the young team of prospects. They lined up eagerly to wait for the well-known former big-league star. As they waited, the guys got talking. The gregarious star had a reputation of being high on himself, and the players were repeating some of the things they had heard him say or do.

One player said the star had wanted to make a point earlier that year in spring training. It seems some of the minor league prospects had gotten a little too cocky, so the star had hoped to bring them back to earth. He had called the young players all around himself, and started asking them how good they thought they were at playing the game of baseball.

"You're good," he asked? "You're real good, aren't you?" Most of them nodded in agreement. The star kept raising the level, poking at their collective confidence level.

"You guys are the best in this league, right?" he said. "Man, you are all the best!" He said, with a tad of sarcasm. Then, in his attempt to bring their egos back into check, he pulled something out of his pocket. "You think you're hot stuff, right? Well, take a look at this." Out of his uniform pocket he pulled a crumpled bank ATM receipt. "Take a look at that, "he boasted. "Look at those six zero's after that comma! And that's just the checking account! When you have those commas and zeros, then you come see me!" With that, the star strutted off toward the clubhouse.

The players stood in relative silence, looking around at each other. Then one player spoke up.

"If he's so smart, why does he have that much in a checking account?"

-Rick Schultz

The Ultimate Baseball Brawl

Most baseball fights are honestly quite lame as far as fights are concerned. There's a lot of pushing a shoving but usually not much else. That wasn't the case in 2003 in a game between Lancaster and Inland Empire in the California League.

It was a late season game with both teams battling for a playoff spot. The game went into extra innings and remained tied into the 15th inning. Inland Empire loaded the bases against Jethawks reliever Josh Kranawetter before a double cleared the bases.

The very next hitter was a Cuban-defector named Evel Bastida, who had left his family behind in Cuba a few years earlier and was drafted by Seattle in 2002. Kranawetter's first pitch sailed behind the back of Bastida. There was almost no question that it was intentional. Bastida charged the mound but unlike every other hitter in this situation, he didn't leave his bat at the plate, rather he took it with him and clocked Kranawetter in the back with bat. The pitcher dropped like he was shot with a 30 odd 6. One of the biggest brawls I've ever witnessed followed the bat attack.

The fight seemed to last forever, with numerous smaller fights breaking out all over the field. Meanwhile, the entire Lancaster team was trying to get to Bastida. I'm sure they would have literally killed him if his teammates weren't able to protect him. They were dragging him down the left field line toward the clubhouse, just trying to get him out of harm's way. Both teams were fighting all the way down the line while the trainers and a couple of coaches were tending to the motionless Kranawetter on the pitcher's mound.

About ½-hour into this fracas, Antelope Valley sheriffs started pulling off the highway and into the stadium. Eventually, order was somewhat restored and the teams were sent to their respective clubhouses, which fortunately were on opposite sides of the stadium.

There was a long delay at this point, maybe 45 minutes, before the inevitable announcement came around midnight that the game would be suspended and finished in San Bernardino a couple of weeks later when Lancaster came to town for a critical series.

Bastida was suspended indefinitely for his actions and would play only one more season in the minors. Inland Empire would hold on to win the completion of the suspended game, which propelled them into the playoffs where they would emerge as California League champions.

-Mike Saeger

Hot-Tempered Man In Blue

I was in my 3rd season in Minor League Ball, calling a road game in the first week of the season. For whatever reason, the team that year was extremely hot-headed, and I think 3-4 guys had been tossed from games before we had even gotten seven games into the season. It all came to a head on this one night.

Still relatively early in the game, the team for which I was working got involved in a close play at the plate. The opposition's throw beat the runner home, but it was off-line in foul territory, and the catcher made an effort to grab it and swing the glove back towards the runner. It looked, from the press box, like the runner had clearly gotten in, but the ump ruled that the catcher had grazed the back of the runner's jersey just before he crossed the plate. The runner was called out, and the whole team went ballistic. The runner slammed his helmet and was immediately tossed; the batter that had doubled to set this whole thing in motion got tossed; the manager came storming down from his perch in the 3rd base coaching box and he got tossed a few seconds later, and between innings a different player yelled something in Spanish that the ump didn't like, and he got tossed, too. Four players in 5 minutes.

Needless to say, emotions were high, and I said something to the effect of, "It seems like a missed call may have just led to almost 20% of the players taking showers, and the umps have lost control of this one." Fairly innocuous, I thought, especially since we're paid by a team that wants things "sugar-coated" just a tad.

30 minutes later I check my email to find a page-long rant about how I can't see [expletive] from the press box and that I'd get my [expletive] [expletive] destroyed if I brought my [expletive] down to the field. Who would be so unprofessional and brash?

Well, apparently one of the two listed umpires for that night's game had to take an emergency flight back to the east coast for a sick relative and the home team's media staff didn't find out, or didn't let me know (or both). So, this angry gentleman was the umpiring partner of the guy that just tossed half a starting lineup, and the other ump was a college replacement.

I still find it absurd that he felt like he had a better grasp of the game from 2500 miles away than I did in the press box, but umpires stick together, sometimes to the point that they lash out at 25-year old broadcasters, and then get lucky that said broadcaster didn't file a complaint.

- Dan Besbris

Close Call at the Border

Following a two-game series in St. Catherine's, Ontario, the 1996 Hudson Valley Renegades were on their bus headed back the United States. As they approached the customs building at the U.S./Canada border, manager Bump Wills stood up and addressed the team in a serious tone.

"No wise comments," he said. "Just keep quiet and let me do the talking."

Teams are occasionally held for a period of time at the border, and nobody wanted a further delay before the 7-hour bus ride home. It had been a long trip, and the mood turned tense as two customs officers boarded the bus and began asking Bump the routine, deadpan questions regarding the bus' occupants.

"Where are you going?"

"Where are you coming from?"

"Are you bringing anything back to the U.S. with you?"

The team had two Spanish-speaking players from the Dominican Republic - flashy right-hander Julio Aquino and his quiet friend, Jose Martinez. Their passports were routinely inspected during trips out of the United States.

Bump called the two pitchers to the front of the bus. As the rest of the players looked on silently, one of the border agents asked Aquino, "Are you Julio Aquino?" At that point, something happened that surprised everyone. Aquino stepped forward, his multi-colored silk shirt unbuttoned down to the chest, with gold chains dangling. He opened his shirt a little more, leaned in, dangled his chains and replied slyly "Si Si Pedro!" This line from the movie "Major League" was one of Aquino's favorites.

The female officer was not amused as the bus erupted into laughter. Wills shook his head with a frown. The officer signaled for Aquino to follow her off the bus and into the customs office. They returned 15 minutes later.

"Let him know that he's very lucky," the officer snapped at Wills. "I could keep you guys here all day if I wanted to! Let the wise guy know that!" She turned and walked down the stairs and off the bus. Bump Wills just shook his head as Aquino bopped back to his seat, getting high-fives from his teammates. The trip home ensued without incident.

-Rick Schultz

Duped in Right Field

Calling a game from behind plate usually provides a full view of the field -- but at times you're at the mercy of judging the outfielders and how they're playing deep fly balls. This is even tougher with younger players still learning the game at the rookie level. In this instance, it is also possible to get duped.

The ballpark was buzzing for a day game on July 4th -- great crowd, but also triple-digit temperatures. In the fourth inning, Billings left fielder Tony Brown, who had a great pull swing to right field, absolutely crushed a pitch towards the fence. It sounded like a goner. I jumped on it -- then watched Helena right fielder Erik Komatsu raise his glove, as if he was preparing to make a catch. There was a pause for a moment -- and then the ball hit the scoreboard! It wasn't just a home run; Brown hit the longest shot of the season. One of the bulbs on the board had to be replaced.

I was completely fooled and felt like I missed the call -- until afterwards, when I spoke to our pitching coach, former Red Tom Browning. He said, "You were fooled? The whole ballpark was!" At least Komatsu had fun with everyone watching in Billings.

-Ed Cohen

What Did He Just Say?

The Western Baseball League was an independent league that operated from 1995 to 2002 and had no affiliation to major league organizations. Two of the league's teams were the Bend Bandits and the Grays Harbor Gulls. Located in Hoquiam, Washington, the Gulls played at antiquated Olympic Stadium.

The all-wood, U-shaped stadium was erected in 1938 and remains a local landmark. In fact, Congressional Representative Norm Dicks' push for the stadium to be added to the National Register of Historic Places was granted in 2005.

During one game early in his career, Doug Greenwald was at the mic as his Bend Bandits played at Grays Harbor in its throwback ballpark. In older venues, such as Olympic Stadium, everyone crams into one tiny press box. Doug was packed tightly into the small booth along with other media members, the public address announcer and other team officials.

The game was coming to a climax in a tense situation, as Greenwald built up the suspense.

"Bottom of the ninth, runners on first and second," he reported. Then, as happens occasionally at 60-year old ballparks, the power went out. "Oh S###!" Greenwald blurted out. The power was out, his equipment was dead, and so he just let out a two-word phrase in frustration, to the laughs of everyone else in the tight booth. Luckily for Doug, the power came back on after only one pitch, and the game resumed.

When the game concluded, Greenwald was chatting with the board operator back in the studio as he packed up his material. "I just want to let you know I heard you say something tonight," the board operator said.

"What do you mean?" Greenwald asked.

"I heard you say a word in the ninth inning," the board op responded. Apparently, even though the power had gone out, Greenwald's backup batteries had maintained his broadcast during the power outage. His listeners hadn't missed a pitch, or a word.

The next morning Greenwald was awoken in his hotel room by a phone call from his station manager.

"I heard what you said last night," the boss told Greenwald.

"Oh," Greenwald responded sheepishly, "I can't lie. I said it. It just happened, I thought the power was out....and I said it."

"Well, you know what I think?" the boss asked. "I think it was actually pretty funny. Just keep an eye on that next time."

A relieved Greenwald hung up the phone and never used that word on the air again.

-Doug Greenwald

Glue

One year my broadcast partner and I dropped into the ballpark to prep our radio booth for the season, which would begin in less than a week. We took some time to tidy up the dusty booth, arrange our table and chairs and test the broadcast equipment.

As usual we joked back and forth about the many "characters" we would encounter during the upcoming season, and we really ripped on one guy in particular. For whatever reason, we were angry at this influential member of the organization, and we bad-mouthed him as we worked. We really didn't care for this front office guy, and we had some pretty colorful things to say about him.

The final task that our station's Director of Sports Development, Bob Outer, gave us was to affix the brand new station sign on the façade directly above our broadcast booth. When fans looked up to the press box, our WBNR sign would hang directly above our booth. There were a few similar windows, and station management wanted fans to know which one was ours.

As instructed, we began to put that shiny, new 3-foot by 4-foot sign up on the press box wall. We laid the sign upside down on the floor and inserted our adhesive caulk into the caulking gun. As we joked about that front office member, we used the caulking gun to let out our frustration. Instead of applying the glue in a zigzag pattern, we wrote a few choice words followed by the front office member's name. Take that! A pair of immature broadcasters had their fun, and the sign looked great as we stuck it above the window of our booth.

We were pumped as we arrived to the ballpark for opening day a week later. As we began to set up our equipment, a ballpark official alerted us that we'd have to change broadcast booths. As the home broadcast team, we were being moved permanently to the next booth over, which was much more spacious. (30 square feet compared to 20) We happily moved our belongings to the next booth.

"Hey guys," said a member of the grounds crew. "Why is your sign above an empty window when you guys are over there?" Oh right, we moved to the next booth but forgot to move the sign on the façade above the window. Luckily we still had the caulking gun, so we began yanking and pulling the sign off the wall. Finally we heard a "Pop" and the plastic sign came down.

"Oh my goodness," my broadcast partner gasped. We both looked up and, to our total shock, we could *clearly* read the horrendous, insulting, crude things we wrote about that front office member. The sign was down, but the glue still spelled those shocking things backwards on the wall – for all 4000 fans to see!

After about ten minutes of absolute panic, we grabbed any small, sharp objects we could find and hurriedly began to chip away at the glue words on the wall. We scraped, yanked and tugged at those vulgar words spelled out in adhesive. Luckily for us, the words began to chip off with determination and a little elbow grease.

Within an hour the words were completely gone. We had averted a crisis that could have derailed a wonderful season before it even began.

-Rick Schultz

Balmy New Jersey

After five losing seasons, the BlueClaws broke through to win the 2006 South Atlantic League title in their sixth season at the Jersey Shore. That meant Opening Day 2007 was going to be one of the most anticipated games in team history, because of the raising of the South Atlantic League Championship Banner.

The team had come up from Florida (to New Jersey) a few days before and I had spoken with Carlos Monasterios, the Opening Day starter. Carlos, the nicest guy in the world, was from Venezuela. He had pitched in the summer leagues there, and the Gulf Coast League, where they play on Florida summer days at 1 in the afternoon. The Phillies had acquired Monasterios from the Yankees in the Bobby Abreu deal the previous summer and this was not only his first time north of Florida, it was his first time in temperatures below 50 degrees. It didn't seem like a huge deal, until he went out to warm up before the 6:35 pm start. It was 32 degrees with snow flurries. Uh oh.

Well, the banner went up at about 6:29 pm. The game started at 6:37 pm. 13 minutes, five hits, a walk, hit batsman, and three wild pitches later, Monasterios' night was over and Greensboro led 7-0. But that banner was really blowing in the wind!

Don't worry about Carlos and the weather. A few years later, the Dodgers selected him in the Rule 5 Draft, and except for a few trips to Colorado, I don't think he spends too much time in sub-50 degree temperatures any more.

-Greg Giombarrese

The Pencil Sharpener

It was my first season with a full-time broadcasting job. I was hired by the Cedar Rapids Kernels of the Midwest League over the winter and couldn't have been more excited to get started. I had interned for the Kernels for two seasons so I was very familiar with the front office staff, the community, the ballpark, and the league.

I had worked under and was replacing John Rodgers, who was a bit of a legend in the Midwest League after spending 15 years behind the microphone in Cedar Rapids. John is the most energetic and personable man I will probably ever met. I will never forget what he did for me in getting my career started. Before interning with John I had done very little work in radio play-by-play broadcasting, but he had the faith in me to give me the opportunity to broadcast numerous games by myself during my two years with him.

Everyone around the league knew John, and John knew everyone around the league. He was known for many interesting traits, including his perfect cursive penmanship with his yellow number-two pencils. John brought his electronic pencil sharpener to every game, home and away during his time in Cedar Rapids.

Our first series of the 2011 season was in Peoria at O'Brien Field. As I made my way into the booth, I noticed an electronic pencil sharpener that was setting on the left of the table. I didn't think anything of it and started to set up my equipment and prepare for the first of 140 games during the season.

Not only did I broadcast my first game of the season in my first full-time gig that night, but I also received my first foul ball in the booth! It was a laser shot that caught me completed off guard, hit the back wall of the broadcast booth, and rested right behind my chair. Getting a foul ball was the last thing from my mind. Many broadcasters go years, or perhaps never get a foul ball into the booth, but I took home a souvenir in game number one.

I had so many other things on my mind that evening. As I scanned the field below from my high perch, I was just trying not to screw anything up! I was more concerned about not missing a play, not mispronouncing a name, not getting so caught up the action that I forgot to speak, and even having enough things to say! The game ended up getting suspended because of rain late in the game. So, I put the foul ball into my bag and rode the bus back to the team hotel.

We came back the following night to complete the suspended game and play the regularly scheduled nine-inning game afterwards. The Kernels would win the suspended game 7-3, by the way. The pencil sharpener was still setting on the table with me as game two got underway.

Shortly into game two, another foul ball came screeching up into the booth! Now, getting a souvenir in my second game was certainly on my mind. But still, what are the odds it would happen two nights in a row, right? This ball came back much quicker than the first one. All I heard was a loud bang! While still trying to maintain my composure on the air, I tried to discover what the ball hit to record such a loud noise! (I still wonder how I didn't utter a swear word on the air while being startled by the ball and trying to save my own life. Had I done so, I may have been fired two games into my broadcasting career!)

The noise was much louder than the night before. Did it again hit the wall behind me? Did it hit off the ledge below the booth and ricochet into the stands below? I spotted the ball off to my left, right next to a shattered pencil sharpener! The pencil sharpener that was setting there through the first two games took a brutal punch from the screeching foul ball! The pencil sharpener shattered into five or six pieces! Pencil shavings were everywhere!

After my heart rate declined to where I wouldn't need to call for an ambulance, I thanked the pencil sharpener for saving my brand new laptop computer that was provided by the Kernels prior to the beginning of the season. If the pencil sharpener had not been setting there, the laptop would have been in five or six pieces. What had I signed myself up for? Who knew radio broadcasting could be so dangerous?

Between innings, Nathan Baliva, Peoria Chiefs radio broadcaster came into the booth to check on me. After laughing about the pencil sharpener, he got me caught up on the story behind the pencil sharpener. Who did it belong to? The one and only John Rodgers, who had left the pencil sharpener there after a series in Peoria in late August of last year!

-Morgan Hawk

20 Minute Triple Play

One of the most unique triple plays in minor league history occurred on the final day of the 1994 New York-Penn League season, in game one of a double-header between the New Jersey Cardinals and Hudson Valley Renegades. The day's action at Skylands Park in New Jersey meant nothing to the Renegades, who were long out of the league race. The Cardinals, meanwhile, were having a great season and had major playoff implications tied to the two games. Depending on what happened in other contests throughout the league, the Cardinals had to win at least one of the two games to make the playoffs. It was ball night at the park, and in game 1 all hell broke loose.

In the bottom of the sixth inning the Cardinals, leading 8-3, had the bases loaded with no outs. On a 2-1 count, Mike Taylor lined a shot down the left field line. The ball dropped toward the ground right on the foul line, just as left fielder Stephen Larkin made a diving attempt. It all happened so fast.

"That ball is....I don't know what it is," said Renegades' radiocaster Bill Rogan. "I don't know if it's fair or foul, and I don't know if it was a catch or not by Larkin!" The umpires made no signal. The Renegades in the field were motionless, simply looking at one another, as Cardinal runners began circling the bases. Two were trying to tag up, one was trying to score, and the umpires still hadn't made any signal or ruling. Guys were all over the place, and not a person on the field knew what was going on. That includes the umpires.

After about fifteen minutes of deliberation, the umps ruled that Larkin had indeed caught the ball in left for the first out of the inning. After a lengthy argument from Cardinals manager Roy Silver, the Renegades decided to appeal to the bases. Throw to first....out! Two down. Appeal to third.....out! A triple play! A 20-minute triple play! That's when it really got ugly at Skylands.

As the Cardinals and their manager argued demonstratively with the umpires, the fans began to fire their baseballs onto the field. Players were simultaneously arguing with the umpires and ducking the whizzing baseballs. Just as fast as the fans launched their baseballs onto the field, the Cardinal players were tossing them back into the crowd.

"If we forfeit the game we blow the playoffs!" implored the public address announcer, trying to calm the chaos. In the midst of the mayhem, one of the thrown baseballs clipped Renegades manager (and future big league coach) Doug Sisson in the leg, and he wasn't the least bit thrilled. The "Sizzler" charged toward the third base stands and went after the fan, soon to be restrained by his team. It took 15 minutes more to calm the crowd down and resume the game, which the Cardinals went on to win. (They eventually also won the New York Penn League Title)

"That may rank number one on the list," Sisson said after the game, calling it one of the wackiest games he'd ever been a part of. "Luckily nothing arose from it. Now I don't have to act like an idiot all winter, because I just got it out of my system."

The real kicker came after the game when, in the locker room, Larkin proclaimed, "I trapped that ball. It wasn't even close!"

-Rick Schultz

Not Just A Radio Guy

In my first season of broadcasting with the Rancho Cucamonga Quakes in 2007, I got to know the players very well. This is something that is not difficult to do seeing that I traveled with the team on the bus and went down to the clubhouse and the field prior to games to talk with the players and coaches. Occasionally, I would notice something with a guy playing particularly well or slumping and would talk to said player about what was going on.

Having the baseball experience that I had (4 year college player and 2003 National Champions in Division III) I felt like I could keep up with these guys and talk mechanics and approach. The players would be taken aback at times because, as some of them said, "You're just a radio guy. You never played the game." Well, I wanted to prove to these guys that I could back up the things that I was talking about and that they weren't just words being spoken, but I had actually played a few thousand games in my life. So, I set up with our manager for me to take batting practice with the team around May (about 6 weeks into the season).

It was the day that I was to take BP and our pitching coach, former big leaguer Ken Patterson (a lefty), said that he would volunteer to throw. Being a left handed hitter, I thought, "Outstanding!" I brought some of my own wood bats with me so that I didn't have to borrow any of the player's game bats. Once the home team was finished hitting, I was already on the field and had taken a couple swings off the tee to get loose.

Our team was stretching in right field when Patterson walked out the field and yelled to me, "Get in there kid. Let's see what you can do." After a few warm up tosses, Patterson was ready and threw three pitches out of the zone to start. A couple players started shouting from the outfield for me to take a swing and getting eager to see what I could do, whether it was good or bad. On the first pitch that was thrown in the strike-zone, a fast ball on the inner part of the plate, I took a swing. I connected....solidly. All of the jeers from the outfield stopped as they looked to the sky and followed the ball as it went over the wall in right field. One swing, one homer, one team in complete shock.

The players then started shouting at me about, "What was that? Where'd that come from? Who is this guy?" I was pretty pleased with myself to say the least. That one swing gave me a little more credibility with my team. I think they gave me the benefit of the doubt from there on out.

I will mention that the next pitch from Patterson after the home run was over my head and the next offering was a nasty breaking ball down and away. I didn't hit another homer in that batting practice session, but it was certainly a moment I'll never forget.

-Jeff Levering

Minor League Turbulence

In 1995, the team was headed into Calgary, which is always known for its air turbulence when you come in for a landing. On this trip, though, we were experiencing the worst turbulence I've ever been on.

Second baseman Brian Raabe was to my left, and says, "Steve, can you turn the fan up all the way? I'm afraid that if I try to reach up my arm I'm going to get sick." So I turn the fan up all the way.
Future major league catcher Damian Miller is on my right, and he says, "Steve, can you lower the shade? I'm afraid if I look outside I'm going to get sick." So I lower the shade.

It was getting pretty tense in the cabin, as we had some guys who were "white knucklers" even on a smooth flight. There was one player, however, who joined the team in mid-season. I would say he is one of the biggest flakes we've had in Salt Lake. In this case, he did not endear himself to his teammates and others on this bumpy ride. You see, every time we hit a pocket of turbulence, he'd raise his arms like he was on a rollercoaster and go "Wheeeeeee!"

Needless to say, many of the guys that were showing some fear on the flight were ready to strangle him as soon as we landed.

-Steve Klauke

Double-Play Breaks Up No-No

In 1994 I witnessed the wackiest ending to a game I've ever seen.

The Hudson Valley Renegades were trailing the New Jersey Cardinals 7-0 in the bottom of the ninth inning, and Renegades were still without a hit. With one out and Dom Gatti on first, future major leaguer Mark Little crushed 2-1 pitch to left. The ball smacked off the top of the wall and was played in quickly to third base. The speedy Little was tagged out sliding into third, and then Gatti was immediately tagged out diving back into third base.

Little broke up the no-hitter by doubling into a double play – to end the game!

-Rick Schultz

Watching from the Dugout

One late August evening in 2008, I was able to step away from my broadcast booth to watch a game from the same view as the players and coaches – the dugout.

Our radio station was carrying a high school football game that night and I knew ahead of time that I wouldn't be on the air. Still, I couldn't see not joining the team on our commuter trip to nearby Cedar Rapids, IA. I had planned on watching the game from my booth – where my equipment was still set up for the remainder of the four-game series – but was given a surprise when the manager asked if I wanted to watch the game from the dugout.

It was a vantage point I had never seen before. Being able to watch a hitter talk to himself and psych himself up for an at-bat down in the tunnel. Watching what the DH does to stay in the game when his teammates are in the field. Seeing how the coaches interact with one another and hearing them continue to teach the players as the game was going on.

I was most surprised by how talkative our starting pitcher was. Pitchers usually have a reputation as being unapproachable in the midst of an outing, but ours was actually sitting next to me during offensive innings, telling me what he was thinking against certain hitters and admiring how solid his stuff was that night. Indeed it was solid, as he allowed just two hits over four innings in what was set to be a playoff tune-up.

I watched from the top step as the LumberKings broke a 1-1 tie in the top of the eighth inning on an RBI single by our star first-baseman, Mitch Moreland. Just two years later, I'd watch that same swing in a Major League game, this time from the familiar perspective of the 35th row.

While I haven't been pre-empted and been able to sit in the dugout for a game since, I find the experience has given me the ability to understand what goes on in a player or coach's mind during a game. It was definitely not what I expected, and it's something I'll never forget.

-Dave Lezotte

A Little Mediocre

After spending a number of years broadcasting minor league baseball, it has been quite a thrill to keep up to date with players I've known, who have moved on and up the baseball ladder. I have had the opportunity to keep in touch with many players over the years - whether in person, by phone, email or simply by following their careers from afar.

Early in the 1999 season I joined a former broadcast partner and travelled down to Salisbury, Maryland to catch a South Atlantic League game at Arthur W. Purdue Stadium. The hometown Delmarva Shorebirds would be playing the Charleston Riverdogs, a Single-A affiliate of the Tampa Bay Devil Rays. Our plan was to make the six-hour drive down, see the game and then drive back in the same day.

The traffic was pretty congested as we crawled through Dover, Delaware on our way to Salisbury, however the trip down was otherwise smooth sailing. We had a terrific time catching up with players and coaches whom we'd gotten to know quite well over the previous few seasons in the Hudson Valley.

We hit the road when the game ended, albeit with our eyes growing a bit weary. It was approaching midnight and, after a short time, we finally accepted the fact that we were going to have to find a hotel. We were just too tired to drive. As we stopped at one hotel and then another, we began to see a trend emerging. There were just no rooms available. The longer we searched, the drowsier we felt.

Finally, at the third try, the hotel manager said there wouldn't be any rooms available for 100 miles because there was a NASCAR event at the nearby Dover International Speedway. Now very tired and dejected, we got back into the car and trudged on.

About a mile up the road we drove past a small, non-descript motel on the right side of the road. As we whizzed by, we both noticed the crooked "Vacancy" sign in bright red lights. Quickly we decided to turn the car around and give it one last shot. We eyed the dingy-looking strip of rooms as we strolled up to the motel office. We were just about to leave after ringing the bell a half a dozen times, when an older gentleman poked his head out the window.

"Hello," he said.

"Do you have any rooms?" we asked.

"Well," he responded hesitantly. "Not really. It's pretty much full." We nodded and started to walk away.

"Oh, alright. We're just getting so tired now. No rooms anywhere," we muttered under our collective breath. "OK, thanks for your time." We were about ten feet down the dusty parking lot when he suddenly called back to us.

"Well, I actually do have one room. It's a little mediocre."

"No problem!" we replied. "We'll take it!" After all, as veteran minor league broadcasters, we had stayed in just about every kind of low-class, fleabag place you could imagine.

"Just give me twenty bucks and I'll show you to the room," the manager said. Surprised and relieved, we gave him the money and he led us across the dusty parking lot to the door. We were so tired at this point, we could have *slept* on that parking lot.

As the manager opened the door, we smelled the stale air. Nothing too bad, but noticeable. We were immediately in the main room, which featured two beds and not much else. The carpet, beds and walls looked a little worn, but not too bad considering how tired and bleary-eyed we had become. We figured "what the heck" and gave the hotel manager the ok. He left and we began getting set for bed.

The stale smell was getting a bit worse, but was still manageable. We both sat on our respective beds and, almost simultaneously, we both rolled to the side and nearly fell off. I got up and looked down at the bed, noticing that it was now distinctly crooked. Both beds were very crooked, and that smell was getting progressively worse. My friend noticed a large, black bug crawling across the floor near his bed, as I decided to head to the bathroom to test out the facilities.

I entered the bathroom and immediately saw a bush growing through the window and down toward the sink! The plant was actually snaking in from outside and branching around the bathroom wall toward the shower. I gasped and raced back to the main room.

"Ouch!" my friend yelled. "I just got bit by something! We just can't stay here!"

We sheepishly rang the manager's bell. He came out holding the $20 bill. He looked at us and said,

"I told you it was a little mediocre."

-Rick Schultz

Ballpark Repair Man

Long before the technical aspects of broadcasting became easier, you had a phone with or without a "voice" coupler and a mic mixer to send the broadcast. I was at a Bill Meyer Stadium (long since torn down) back in the early 90's to broadcast the series between the Lookouts and the Smokies.

Having been schooled by my father as well as the radio biz regarding "anything can happen so be ready" knowledge, the phone I was to use wasn't working. The team didn't have a backup and it was the weekend so I knew it was up to me to find a way to get it to work. I unscrewed the mouth piece and discovered one of the wires was not connected where it should be. Seeing it had solder on the end of the wire I used a lighter to heat the solder and repair the connection. The phone had a dial tone and the broadcast went on. I informed the club about the need for a new phone or to fix the one that I had used. They agreed and would look into it.

The following season I was at the same location and curiosity prompted a peek at the inside of the phone as it looked like the same one I had used previously. My soldering job was still intact after the previous season of use and a couple of months into the new one.

Just goes to show that using the brain first to solve a problem is the best way to stay out of trouble.

- Larry Ward

Detour To The Big Leagues

Outfielder Trayvon Robinson was a hot Dodgers prospect playing with Triple-A Albuquerque in 2011. He was having a breakout season, posting career highs in homeruns (26), runs batted in (71), and slugging percentage (.563) through 100 games.

A lifelong Dodger fan, Tray grew up in Compton in South Central L.A., went to the same high school, Crenshaw, as Darryl Strawberry, Ellis Valentine, and Chris Brown, all big league all-stars.

In mid-July, Dodger manager Don Mattingly said Robinson definitely would play in L.A. at some point in 2011, but the Dodgers traded Tray at the July 31st deadline, literally.

I was sitting with Tray on the shuttle bus outside the team hotel in New Orleans, waiting to head to Zephyr Field for the Isotopes game that day. That's when he got the phone call, exactly one minute before the deadline.

Tray stepped off the bus, so he could hear better, so he could confirm the news, collect his thoughts. You could tell he was heartbroken, his team, HIS team, the Dodgers, had traded him. The first phone call revealed he'd been sent to Boston, but he was told to keep his phone close by.

For a couple minutes, he thought he was going to the Red Sox. Then, another call, and the news Boston had dealt him to Seattle in a three-team trade, the Red Sox receiving pitcher Erik Bedard from the Mariners to fortify their rotation for the stretch run.

I interviewed Tray that afternoon, his head spinning, his heart a twisted bundle of emotions. If you listened carefully, you could almost hear tears as his voice cracked a couple times.

Tray joined Seattle's Triple-A team, Tacoma, and actually played against his old team, the Isotopes, in Albuquerque a couple days later. He even met the new Dodger catching prospect Tim Federowicz, for whom Tray was traded, acquired from Boston as the centerpiece of the deal for L.A. They shared a laugh over fate's funny way of bringing them together.

Seattle called up Tray while Tacoma was in Albuquerque, after just three games with the Rainiers. All his old teammates and friends were still with the Isotopes, and Tray celebrated the proudest moment of his professional career.

He debuted for Seattle the next night in Anaheim, about 20 miles from where he grew up, with his Mom, a big Angels fan, in the stands. In his debut, Tray robbed all-star and gold glove outfielder Torii Hunter of a two-run homerun, leaping into the seats to pull it back. It was Tray's first appearance on ESPN Sportscenter's Top 10 plays.

Tray notched his first hit that night, then homered the next day in Anaheim, his first in the Bigs. One month later, Tray hit his second homerun, once again in Anaheim, to remind L.A. that its hometown boy was doing okay.

-Robert Portnoy

Geography Lesson

During a humid afternoon in the 1999 season I caught a cab from a barbeque restaurant in Oneonta, New York, along with a couple of the Hudson Valley Renegades. We were cramped three across the back seat, headed back to the team hotel and chatting about some of the recent trips we had taken.

"Remember we played in Utica," a Dominican-born player said in broken English. "Is that where they play basketball?" The rest of us just looked at him, a little confused because he didn't speak much English. He was referring to the Utica Blue Sox in central New York State. Again he asked, and again we just looked at him, because we didn't' understand what he meant. He was a terrific pitcher and jovial guy, but very difficult to understand.

"Utica was the Blue Sox," we said.

"They play basketball?" he responded quizzically, "You know, Stockton, Malone?"

At last we realized he meant *Utah*, as in the Utah Jazz with superstars Karl Malone and John Stockton, and not *Utica*. There is no NBA team in quaint Utica, NY. He was all smiles after we explained the difference and cleared up his confusion.

-Rick Schultz

Blinded By The Light

I learned well before the Boston media and even the national press that David Ortiz had a great sense of humor. He spent almost the entire 1999 season in a Salt Lake Buzz uniform and put together some great numbers, a sign of great things to come; hitting .315 with 30 homers and 110 runs batted in. Unfortunately, Ortiz also showed why he eventually made his mark as a designated hitter. He set and still owns the Salt Lake franchise record for most errors in a season by a first baseman with twenty.

One day, David was taking some extra batting practice, so I wandered near the cage. After about three or four minutes of struggling to make good contact, Ortiz stopped what he was doing and set his bat down on home plate. Next thing I know, he walks around the cage, takes his hat off and puts it on my head. Ortiz proceeds to tell me that the glare was bothering him.

-Steve Klauke

Give Us A Wave

Minor League ballplayers come in all varieties. Some are loud and boisterous, others are quiet and reserved. Some view broadcasters with skepticism, while others treat the team radiocaster as he would any other teammate. One of the real good guys in the latter category was utility man extraordinaire Alex Llanos of the 1998 Hudson Valley Renegades.

Throughout the 1998 season, Bill Rogan and I went back and forth with Llanos, asking him when he was going to wave to us in the radio booth. He often told us he saw us up there, working hard during the games. "Why not give us a wave?" we asked.

One day late in the season, the Renegades were playing against the Vermont Expos at Centennial Field in Burlington, Vermont. It was a tight, late-inning situation. Hudson Valley had a runner on and desperately needed to get him into scoring position. The large crowd watched with anticipation as Alex Llanos strolled to the plate. The tension was really building as the pitcher came set and stared in at Llanos.

Then, out of the blue, Alex Llanos held out his hand and asked the home plate umpire for time. He stepped out of the batters box, looked way up to our booth behind home plate, and gave us a big, sweeping wave. Bill and I lost it on the air, laughing hysterically.

Llanos then laid down a perfect sacrifice bunt and gave us another look as he jogged off the field into the dugout.

-Rick Schultz

Innings, Innings And More Innings

Doug Greenwald once called 35 innings in just two days. He was broadcasting for the Shreveport Swamp Dragons of the Texas League, when the team played back-to-back marathon affairs against San Antonio and Tulsa.

On July 2, 2001, Shreveport lost a tough one in 17 innings at San Antonio. (The longest minor league game in history came in 1981, when the Pawtucket Red Sox edged the Rochester Red Wings 3-2 in 33 innings. Still, 17-inning games are very rare.) Following the loss, the team showered, packed up, and journeyed home to Louisiana, where they arrived at 8:30 a.m. That night they began a home series with the Tulsa Drillers, a Texas Rangers affiliate.

The Swamp Dragons were understandably tired to start the ballgame that night. Manager Bill Russell was ejected from the game in the fifth inning, trying to light a spark under his sluggish team. It seemed to work, as Shreveport fought through the fatigue and forced a second straight night of extra innings. Both clubs received excellent pitching in the extra frames, and the game remained tied into the 15th inning! However, Shreveport had a problem. After playing so many innings the night before, they were now flat out of pitchers. Catcher Guillermo Rodriguez was behind the plate the previous night in San Antonio, and in the 15th he was called on *to pitch* for Shreveport. Against a Tulsa team featuring Hank Blalock and Kevin Mench, many thought it was all but over for Shreveport. Amazingly, Rodriguez held the Drillers scoreless for three innings!

In the 18th inning, Shreveport turned the ball over to first baseman Jeremy Lester, who had never pitched in Little League, High School or any level of baseball. He gave up two in the 18th and Tulsa went on to win. Bill Russell, who had been tossed and sent to the showers in the 5th, told Doug Greenwald the worst part of the extra inning loss was having to come back to the clubhouse and listen for 13 innings to his broadcast. For Greenwald, it had been 35 innings of play by play and two losses in two days.

-Doug Greenwald

The .338 Hitter

It is quite extraordinary to see a career .338 big league hitter trying to pick up tips from minor leaguers. Perhaps the continuous desire to improve is precisely what helps propel one to Cooperstown. Regardless, it is not something you see at a ballpark every day.

During the summer of 1998, the Hudson Valley Renegades played a special game against the Pittsfield Mets at Shea Stadium in New York. The game was followed by the big league contest featuring the San Diego Padres and the New York Mets. The minor league game was a warm up for the day's big league action, although it was certainly a career highlight for just about every minor leaguer on either team.

As the minor leaguers battled it out, most of the big leaguers were undoubtedly nestled cozily in their plush clubhouse, if at the ballpark at all. One player in particular, however, was fully dressed and watched the minor league game from the dugout. 2007 Hall of Fame inductee Tony Gwynn spent much of the game on the Renegades' bench; sharing stories, insight and advice.

"It's fun for me because I think for most of the guys playing in the big leagues, playing in the minor leagues was a fun experience," Gwynn reminisced. "Having an opportunity to sit on the bench and talk to the guys, guys coming up to you and asking questions, you kind of re-live your minor league days."

The affable Gwynn clearly hadn't forgotten his days in the bush leagues. He joked and offered advice to the players, imparting many helpful lessons he had learned over the years.

"I know it's tough. In the big leagues we're spoiled rotten," he said with a smile. "We get gloves, shoes, whatever we need, and you see these minor leaguers walking around and their spikes are worn down, almost to the sole of their shoes. And for me it's just a lot of fun hanging out with them and being able to relay stories about when I came up."

Perhaps the most astonishing reason for him spending the game on the bench with the minor leaguers shouldn't be that surprising after all.

"I'm a little selfish too," he admitted. "I come out and I watch guys hit and maybe by watching other guys hit I can pick up some things I might be doing, because mechanically I'm having a lot of trouble right now. So I saw a lot of guys today doing things right; the way it should be done." Gwynn hit .321 in 1998, yet he was analyzing the swings of minor leaguers for any pearls for improvement.

The game lost a true gentleman when Tony Gwynn passed away in 2014. His career was built on hard work, class and a constant desire to share and help others improve. And on that summer day at Shea Stadium – through his generosity and insight – Tony Gwynn gave a team full of minor leaguers a baseball memory they'll never forget.

-Rick Schultz

The Bathroom Delay

One of the challenges a minor league broadcaster faces is filling airtime during delays. Unlike our major league counterparts, who have broadcast partners and studio hosts, the minor league radio man is truly a one man band. I always keep an eye on the weather forecast, to have taped interviews accessible if a rain delay is pending.

Sometimes, the delays can't be forecasted. I improvised through a sudden darkness delay when the lights went out in Portland, Oregon. I read scores and grabbed guests when the sprinklers came on and wouldn't stop in Provo, Utah. But the delay that truly froze me on the air was the one I talked through in June of 2007, when the game was halted for a "bathroom delay" in Montgomery, Alabama.

Mobile pitcher Matt Elliott pitched the eighth inning, but didn't take the field with his teammates for the top of the ninth inning. If he was injured, another pitcher would have begun warming up, but the bullpen mound was empty. Mobile's manager Brett Butler was talking to the home plate umpire, shrugging his shoulders and scratching his head. Our commercial break was over, the inning was about to start, and there was no pitcher in sight. Something was askew here.

After a few minutes of speculating, I received a note in the press box saying "Elliott locked in bathroom." I was hesitant to give this news on the air, fearing I may be a victim of a practical joke, but when I peeked into the Montgomery radio booth, their team's voice nodded and confirmed it was true. Stadium employees said Elliott slammed the door in frustration after allowing the tying run in the eighth inning.

A new pitcher scurried in for Mobile and Montgomery eventually won the game in extra innings, but Elliott wasn't there to see it. He was locked in the bathroom until 20 minutes after the game, and the local fire department had to come and pry the door open!

-Tim Hagerty

Man In Blue

During a game in 1998, Renegades relief pitcher Jon Cummins accomplished a feat that is difficult to comprehend in professional baseball. Midway through the game, Cummins was summoned to take over for an injured umpire who had to leave the game. One player from each team was picked to umpire when their team was on defense, while the only other umpire remained behind home plate. For a player who hadn't officiated anything other than soccer and a few little league games, it was a wacky memory he won't soon forget.

Midway through the ballgame when one of the two umpires was hurt, both managers were called out to home plate. After a lengthy discussion with the one remaining ump, they each returned to their respective dugouts. The Renegades' pitching coach and former big leaguer, Ray Searage, called down the bench to Cummins.

"He said they needed me to umpire," Cummins recounted. "I said 'Are you serious?'"

Tampa Bay Devil Rays field coordinator, Tom Foley, leaned over and asked, "You do know what you are doing, don't you?"

Cummins had a pretty good idea and responded, "I can't believe I'm going it to umpire a minor league baseball game." Cummins said it was a surreal experience. "It was a little different being on the other side of both teams. I saw some of the different things they go through. Usually standing on the hill looking down at the catcher and the umpire, you don't really think about it that much. I was nervous at first. What if I have to make a close call and everybody's arguing and the coach comes out to get in my face?"

Cummins was lucky enough to have an uneventful few innings as an acting umpire and, ironically, later came in to pitch three effective innings. One blemish on his line, however, was a home run he allowed as a result of a *blown call by the umpire*. The ball actually hit the top of the wall in left center, but the home plate ump thought it had hit the scoreboard and caromed back into the field. After umpiring in the same game, Cummins didn't feel right putting up much of an argument.

"I was hoping he'd give me a call," Cummins joked. "Since we were pals out there now."

One would expect the wacky experience would give this pitcher a newfound respect for the men in blue. "A little bit," he surmised. "But you know how that goes. You can't like the umpires. Win or lose, either way they are bad. But they do a pretty tough job out there."

-Rick Schultz

Deer Crossing

To sum it up, we were heading from Burlington, VT to Troy, NY a trip that is supposed to take about 2.5 hours. However, our bus driver, who will stay unnamed (haha), got lost several times, taking nothing but mostly side streets and streets with traffic lights the entire way there-no highways. We came to multiple dead ends in the wee hours of the morning on the trip that followed a night game. One of the dead ends was an old wooden bridge that was too narrow for the bus to fit, so we had to turn around and find another way. Just about an hour after that, we were cruising along a one way road in the middle of the woods when a deer popped up in the middle of the road. Our hitting coach started screaming, "deer, deer, DEEERRR!!!" The driver did not notice until the last second, veered to the left, the deer strolled to his left and BANG! Our bus absolutely crushed the deer, hitting him head on! The entire bus let out a loud gasp, followed by a series of laughs. Our trainer, the driver and our manager got off the bus to check out the damage, but thankfully no damage done to the bus, except for the damage of the deer, OUCH! So we were on our way.
About a mile down the road there were a couple young girls walking on the side of the road. He did not seem to see them and the entire bus screams, "People, people, PEOPLEEEE!!!" However, this time luckily he missed them by just inches, with the one friend pulling her other friend out of the road just in the nick of time. This brought on tons of laughs and jeers from the players!
We finally made it into the hotel at Troy, NY about 4.5 hours later, 2 hours more than the usual trip there from Burlington. I now get the shivers whenever I think of that sound of our bus nailing the deer! One unforgettable bus trip that is for sure, gotta love the life of minor league baseball, what an adventure it is!

-Justin Sheinis

Never Second-Guessing

Most ethical broadcasters would agree that overly critical second-guessing has no place in a broadcast. First-guessing - before the fact - absolutely! In other words, giving your educated opinion on what a manager or player should do before the play is fine. Giving no opinion and then ripping him after the fact should be done rarely, and only in specific situations.

First-guessing is a perfect opportunity for a broadcaster to think along with a manager and voice his opinions aloud for the listener. Nowhere in a broadcast is there any better spot to show just how smart a baseball man you are. Voice your opinion before the play, and see how things transpire.

I was one of the smartest broadcasters in the New York Penn League in 1998. When the opposing team had multiple runners on base against Hudson Valley, I had a knack for being prescient and predicting what may follow – a pickoff attempt, a pitchout, step off the mound, etc. With impeccable clairvoyance, I was able to give my opinion about what should happen, and then watch it actually happen a few seconds later. To my loyal listeners, perhaps I seemed like a baseball genius.

The secret to my uncanny success? Was I a secret descendant of Casey Stengel, Connie Mack or John McGraw? Implanted with a top-secret baseball microchip? Able to ride a time machine with Michael J. Fox? Nope. I had become very friendly with second baseman Dustin Carr who, over time, let me in on the team's signals. It wasn't exactly like passing along the nuclear codes, and he also knew I wasn't going to run my mouth to the rest of the New York Penn League. A very loyal and ethical guy himself, Carr didn't exactly volunteer the signs to me. Over time, however, I worked him down enough to figure out what they were.

As a result, when catcher Toby Hall stepped out in front of home plate to give signals to his defense, he was also giving them to his broadcaster. I knew what the defense might do before they did it. In these instances I never had to second-guess, because my first guess was always correct!

As first baseman Chick Gandil said in "Eight Men Out", "If you don't play the angles, you're a sap."

For much more info about "Never Second Guessing," and to join our Online Sports Broadcasting course for just $10, vist: Udemy.com/sportscasting (Use promo code JUST10)

-Rick Schultz

The Aberdeen Letdown

In 2008, I was a group sales and marketing intern with the Aberdeen IronBirds (Short-season A affiliate of the Baltimore Orioles), working for Ripken Baseball. All summer, my incentive for working the Minor League grind in the Maryland humidity, aside from my palpable passion for the game of baseball and working for my childhood hero, was to make my way back into the radio booth after serving as the number two broadcaster for the Frederick Keys (High-A, Baltimore Orioles) during their championship run a season earlier.

After reaching my sales goal during the height of the season, one of my fill-in assignments was to broadcast a matchup against the Hudson Valley Renegades at Ripken Stadium with play-by-play man, Steve Melewski, former Voice of the IronBirds, and current contributor to the Orioles Radio Network. Melewski was only in Aberdeen for the one broadcast due to his other responsibilities in Charm City.

As a die-hard Orioles fan myself, this was a huge opportunity to do a game with one of the O's voices I had followed as a kid. Melewski showed up about an hour-and-a-half before game time on a beautiful night in Aberdeen. In preparation for his arrival, all of my pre-game scripts and notes were complete and I looked forward to serving as a fly-on-the-wall to watch a perennial professional go about his business.

Over a few sandwiches and fixings from the club level grille, the gregarious Melewski and I chatted about everything baseball…the state of the Orioles, the challenges of a young aspiring broadcaster in professional baseball, and Melewski's whole-hearted enthusiasm in recounting his first Orioles broadcast. It was the perfect start to a memorable broadcast in Aberdeen. Unfortunately, the night was memorable for the wrong reason.

The IronBirds are well known in the minors for consistency in selling out their home contests, and this night was no different. In front of a packed gallery at "The House that Ripken Built," Melewski and I began to voice the pre-game show atop the sun-soaked diamond, and I was gearing up for this atypical night of baseball banter. Two breaks into our scene setting, my heart abruptly sunk, as the Baltimore broadcasting staple to my left pointed out that the Renegades must have gotten no sleep on their latest bus trip, because they were nowhere to be found. There were no red jerseys coming out of the visiting clubhouse, and now it occurred to me, I hadn't seen any Hudson Valley players warming up in any fashion amidst my enamored conversation with my new colleague. In fact, not even the visiting team bus was visible to my fellow raconteur, who was pointing to where it usually resides.

After much deliberation and inquisition within the press box, it was confessed that the Hudson Valley bus had in fact, broken down on Interstate 95. Melewski and I tried to make the best of it and laugh off the fact that you never know what you're going to see at a baseball game, even grabbing the binoculars I still have to this day, and searching down I-95 for the stranded motor coach with no avail. And on this night, because of theatrics we will never know underneath the hood of a visiting bus, the IronBirds would get to rest in their nest before the sun set in the west. Inevitably the game was cancelled and my broadcast with Steve Melewski came to a premature conclusion.

My dejected expression was hard to cover up, and disappointment washed over my face as I shook Melewski's hand and thanked him for his kindness and career advice. He looked back at me with the cool demeanor of a veteran who was thinking, "Sometimes that's the way it goes." It was a lonely stroll through the Ripken Stadium concourse to my truck that night. I was surrounded by the soundtrack of the loyal IronBirds following who were also mourning the loss of one of their home games. My discontent would dull slightly, however, when my father provided a dose of reasoning over the phone. He reminded me it was an invaluable experience to meet and share the radio booth with a Major League caliber talent, and even if the ride was short-lived, that I should prepare for the next opportunity that comes along. Three front offices later, it proves Dad was right.

I have crossed paths with Steve Melewski many times since the debacle, and I look forward to his conversations every time. He's a great broadcaster and a terrific guy. And thus, within my own theater of mind, I still think about what could have been before the Aberdeen letdown.

- Bryan Holland

Pizza Man

One of the many unique aspects of minor league baseball is the way teams and local businesses team up to create fun and memorable contests during the game. For example, in 1999 a pizza restaurant teamed with the Hudson Valley Renegades to sponsor the "K-Man" promotion. One member of the visiting team would be selected each game to be the "K-Man". If he struck out three times, everyone in attendance would win a free pizza.

During this particular game, Lowell Spinners 17-year-old shortstop Cesar Saba was chosen as the night's K-Man. Going into the sixth inning, the Dominican shortstop was 0 for 3 with two strikeouts. The game was tied 5-5 when Saba came up for a fourth time, and the fans were going ballistic. Derek Anderson dealt.....strike one! The fans let out cheers as if they had just won the title. Pitch...strike two! The crowd of 4183 was on their feet. The pitch....strike three! Anderson had struck out Saba and won free pizzas for everyone in attendance!

The next afternoon, one of the Renegades saw Saba, who asked, "Why did they keep yelling Pizza Man at me?" Saba spoke very little English and had no idea what all the excitement was about. The player explained what the contest was all about.

That night some fans greeted Saba with "Hey Pizza Man!" and he handled it with a gracious smile. Hopefully someone gave him a pizza or two for his efforts.

-Rick Schultz

Tense Elevator Ride

In 1995, Buzz manager Phil Roof had me keep track of the team's wins and losses based on who was the home-plate umpire. I said, "Well, I'll do it, but don't ever bring it up to an umpire."

Well there was an umpire who is currently in the big leagues, Ted Barrett, and that season the Buzz were 2-17 when he was behind the plate. So he made a call that Phil thought was a bad call in the playoff series in Vancouver, and Phil tells him, "Our radio guy says we're 2-17 when you're behind the plate."

The next day I come back from lunch and hit the elevator button and the doors open and there are the four umpires. And I get in and the one guy goes, "So, I hear you keep track of what the won-lost record for your team is based on who the home-plate umpire is." Needless to say, I felt very uncomfortable at that point until Barrett and his crew started to chuckle. I laughed, as well, but it was a nervous laugh, at best.

-Steve Klauke

Roger, Roger, Roger

Roger LaFrancois was a career .400 hitter in the major leagues. He went 4 for 10 as a backup catcher with the 1982 Boston Red Sox. I met him in 1998 when he was the manager of the Pittsfield Mets in the Class-A New York-Penn League and I was the team's radio play-by-play guy. They say when you work in the minor leagues, you meet some colorful characters. Roger was one of them.

There was the night of the fireworks show in Pittsfield when Roger got ejected for arguing with the umpire. Earlier that day, because of the overflow crowd, one of the resourceful members of the front office had asked the staff to find extra chairs anywhere they could. This apparently included the clubhouse. All of the players' chairs at their lockers, and even the manager's chair from his office, were removed. So there's Roger, ejected in the early innings, pacing in the clubhouse ... with nowhere to sit!

An absolute classic, though, was a game in New Jersey against the Cardinals when Roger went out to argue a disputed ground-rule double. A Cardinals player hit a drive to centerfield that clearly bounced over the wall and hit the fence beyond the outfield wall. The Mets centerfielder Allen Dina raised his hand to indicate it should be a ground-rule double. The umpire missed the call and the batter advanced to third base for a triple. Roger was furious! He sprints out to second base, and after a raging argument, asks Mets' shortstop Kenny Miller to give him the baseball. I'll show these guys there are two walls back there, Roger was apparently thinking. He loads up from just behind the second base bag and throws the ball over the wall. It doesn't come back. It hits the second fence and bounces down. See, Roger thinks, that's my point! Of course, he's ejected. But it doesn't end there.

After being thrown out, he walks to the Mets' bullpen down the leftfield line. Why? The clubhouse is down the rightfield line. It takes a couple of pitches, but the umpire eventually notices Roger sitting on the bullpen bench and ejects him again! And he's still not done! Roger climbs the fence and goes into the picnic area! There he is, having a hot dog with some fans as the game continues. Only in the minor leagues!

-Connell McShane

Kangaroo Court

Kangaroo Court is a fun minor league ritual that allows players to have fun with one another and let off some steam. The basic idea is that any member of the team can be "fined" by another team member, for doing anything that "embarrasses the team".

For example, perhaps you tripped and fell exiting the team bus. One player was "fined" for "being a politician", as he was always seen holding babies while signing autographs before games. Another player was fined for sneaking off to the clubhouse to call his girlfriend on the phone during a rain delay.

One New York Penn League broadcaster was fined for drinking a cheap beer, the only kind he could afford. One team levied, and collected, multiple fines on their bus driver for all of his wrong turns. Your clothes, your behavior, something you say – all fair game to get yourself fined in Kangaroo Court.

There are no official rules for how to conduct the Kangaroo Court. The fines are usually less than $10, and – usually during rain delays – the team will hold court to allow team member to fight the charges. A senior member of the team usually takes the duty of judge to keep the proceedings moving. The Kangaroo Court is an amusing way to keep things light, and the total pot of money collected from the fines is often used for an end-of-season party. Some teams include support staff and even radio broadcasters as well.

While broadcasting for Shreveport in 2001, Doug Greenwald was unexpectedly included in the club's Kangaroo Court. The team had finished a late night affair in Wichita, and Greenwald headed out along to the only restaurant in town. As he strolled up to the bar to order some dinner, he noticed many members of the Shreveport team tucked away in a back corner room. Doug thought nothing of it, ate his dinner, and left.

The next day Greenwald got brought up in Kangaroo Court, on charges that he "showed up to a party he wasn't invited to." As is customary, he was able to provide his own defense. "First, if I had known you guys were there having a party, I wouldn't have come," he said sharply. "Second, I didn't come over to join you. And third, where the heck else could I have gone to eat?"

After a few minutes of deliberation, the judge came back with his ruling.

"Doug is right," the judge ruled. "Where else would he eat?"

The judge, in turn, fined the accusing players instead!

-Doug Greenwald

King of the Throne

Minor league broadcasters are often loners. Many minor league clubs, especially at the lower levels, employ only one broadcaster to handle their entire radiocast. Where the big leagues are flush with entire crews, consisting of play by play men, color analysts, sideline hosts, producers and engineers, minor league broadcasters often handle the entire production themselves. When flying solo, minor league broadcasters must do everything in their power to prepare for three, or more, consecutive hours on the air. The biology involved is one of the first – and most painful – lessons a broadcaster must learn.

The "old" Dwyer Stadium in Batavia, New York was built in 1939. It was one of those wooden ballparks out of baseball's golden era, with rickety bleachers and a small town charm. For broadcasters, however, the park didn't exactly offer a plethora of comforts and amenities. For one, the broadcast booth was perched high above the home plate grandstand, and could only be accessed by climbing a ladder up through a hold in the roof. The small press box consisted of three rooms – one for the scorekeeper and scoreboard operator, one for home radio and one for the visiting radio team. Inside each booth were a wooden table and a garbage receptacle.

Very similar to the press box at historic Wahconah Park in Pittsfield, Massachusetts, a broadcaster could feel very much in his own world, situated high above the grandstand here in Batavia. Perhaps that's why the home broadcast booth had a distinct scent. The desperate smell of a panicked broadcaster calling an extra-inning game after a few too many soft drinks. Even broadcasters have limits.

Dwyer Stadium was torn down after the 1995 season, and replaced with a shiny, new and sweet smelling ballpark by the same name.

Russell Diethrick Park in Jamestown, New York was opened in 1941, although it doesn't share the same issue that plagued the original Dwyer Stadium. Very much the opposite, actually. The press box at Diethrick Park also sits atop the grandstand; however it features numerous rooms and 12 windows that peer out onto the field. In fact, one of those rooms is a restroom. In one of the great, hidden secrets of minor league baseball, broadcasters have been able to "sit" comfortably, while looking out over live action on the field. Who says minor league life isn't glamorous?

Long road trips are especially precarious in this regard. Picture 3 a.m., you're in the second row of a bus filled with baseball prospects. Most everyone is sleeping, with arms, legs and other body parts draped across and over seats. (Occasionally a player will even crawl into the overhead storage compartment in an attempt to spread out for some shut-eye.)

Anyway, it's the middle of the night and the restroom is all the way at the back of the bus. Let's just say it's not easy to climb over and under those 25 players on the way back to the lavatory, with the bus weaving to and fro. One slip, and that could be some guy's pitching arm you land on. One false move, and you're landing head first on a backup catcher. These are the real perils of minor league baseball.

-Rick Schultz

Minor League Thief

Never have I had a bigger scare and a tougher situation to navigate through as a broadcaster than in 2007 with the Burlington Royals. In the Appalachian League, we usually traveled early in the morning to start a road series that night. In this case in late July, we opened a six-day road trip in Bristol, Virginia, against the White Sox affiliate. Upon arriving at the Howard Johnson hotel, I checked into my room, taking my luggage and notes with me, but as I eventually learned, leaving the box with all of the radio equipment just outside the door. Sure enough, maybe 10 minutes later, I realized something was missing -- the equipment was gone!

I raced around the hotel, filed a police report, made tens of phone calls, screamed to the heavens -- I even made an announcement to the players on the loudspeaker on the bus. Like a ballplayer without a bat and glove, I was torn, and on the road no less. Around 5 o'clock, reality set in: accept the sorrows of a disastrous day...or get ready to call a game! Ultimately, I rallied to call a 6-4 Sox win using a landline phone, holding the receiver to my ear the entire time...in hindsight, it was one of my best accomplishments as an announcer, given what had happened earlier in the day.

Thankfully the game was quick -- just two hours and eighteen minutes -- and the staff in the press box was extremely kind in not charging for a long distance call. Same for the folks who helped out for the final five days of the trip. I also made the local paper the next day -- the team's beat writer, ironically named Bucky Dent, said it wasn't just a bad night for the Royals, but their announcer, too.

-Ed Cohen

The Peach Pit

The Hudson Valley Renegades played in the New York-Penn League's McNamara division along with, among others, the New Jersey Cardinals. Both teams opened similar new ballparks in 1994, and Hudson Valley and New Jersey quickly developed an extremely heated rivalry - included brawls, melees between players and fans and some terrific, dramatic ballgames. For broadcasters, however, it is the small things that sometimes create the long-standing memories.

The Renegades played at Skylands Park in New Jersey six times per season. During our first trip to Skylands one year, we noticed a peach pit in the press box elevator. For whatever reason, this humored us. Being baseball broadcasters, it often didn't take much.

The funny thing was that each time we returned to Skylands Park for another ballgame, the peach pit was still there. Six trips to New Jersey, and my mind tells me that peach pit never moved. Not one inch from its spot on that elevator floor. As silly as it sounds, we actually discussed the peach pit on the way to those games.

"I bet we'll see the peach pit!"

"Yes, I wonder if it's still there."

An inconsequential little peach pit, and it became a running joke throughout the three-month season. Perhaps baseball broadcasters have a little too much time on their hands.

-Rick Schultz

Tinkle Tinkle

The first baseball game I ever broadcast was in April, 2006. I was filling in on radio for the Rancho Cucamonga Quakes home broadcast because their regular #1 guy moved over to TV for that particular game. I had gone to college with the Quake Public Address announcer and he gave me a heads up that they may need someone to fill in on Saturdays because of their TV deal. The Quakes called me at midnight the day prior to the game and I was ecstatic to make my baseball debut.

A little back story…I had never called a baseball game prior to this day. I had done football, basketball, softball, lacrosse, soccer, volleyball…everything but baseball, but the one thing I did have was playing experience. I played ball all the way through college, so at least I knew the game enough to talk about it.

Typical of Southern California , normally a 75 minute drive took me three hours, but I left plenty early to be on time regardless. As soon as I walked into the press box, I got nervous. So much so that I just began drinking bottles of water like I was sponsored by Arrowhead Water Company! I was so nervous about being prepared enough that I completely neglected to use the restroom before I began the pregame show. About the 7th inning and 10 bottles of water down in what was already a really long game, I started to feel a bit uncomfortable with the amount of water that was trying to make it through my body.

Because we only have 60-second breaks between innings and the fact I was doing the game solo, I didn't have the time to run to the restroom between innings. It was the top of the 8th and the Quakes pitchers hit a wall. No one was throwing strikes. When they did throw a strike, it would be hit. No one on defense was catching the ball. All the while I'm standing up in the back row of the press box doing "the pee-pee dance" to try and get the sensation away from my body.

After the second pitching change of the inning (and with the radio format I was using, there were no breaks for pitching changes…no fill, no time to put the headset down), I couldn't handle it any more. I grabbed one of the 24 oz. empty bottles from the desk I was sitting at and relieved my situation…still on the air, still mid-inning, still trying to make sense of this awful game people were subjecting themselves to. I filled the whole bottle and I was a changed man! Luckily, the place where I was seated was separated from the rest of the people in the room. Yes, throughout this entire ordeal, I was sharing talking space with the TV broadcasters, the newspaper writer, the visiting radio broadcaster, the scoreboard operator and the official scorer in a 10'x25' room. No one had a clue, thankfully, and I was able to conceal the filled bottle so that no one would ever know.

I made it through my first broadcast, thanked the Quakes for the opportunity and ditched the bottle without anyone ever knowing what had ever happened! I go back and listen to the tape of that game every now and again and the pain in my voice from the 7th inning until the 8th is laughable. But, once all was said and done, I finished the game, even got a few compliments from listeners and thus started my baseball broadcasting career. Ever since that day, I always use the restroom prior to the game!

-Jeff Levering

Be Careful What You Say

One fun aspect of radio in the minors is that many ballparks will pipe the live game broadcast throughout the ballpark, parking lot and team offices. This can be both a blessing and a curse. On one hand, it's great for fans to be able to hear the live action as they visit the restrooms, concession stands or parking lot. On the other hand, over the course of an entire season, a broadcaster is bound to say something someone won't like. Once, or maybe a thousand times. You can't make everyone happy, and no matter how many positive things you say, you'll always hear about the one negative comment you made.

For example, one year during a day game my broadcast partner commented when the team's big, lumbering first baseman reached first with a walk.

"Don't worry," he said. "Martinez is not a threat to steal. He runs as if he's wearing ankle weights."

A few innings later the game was delayed by rain, and we began some rain-delay banter to fill time. While we went back and forth, we looked down to see that Martinez had walked all the way around to the screen behind home plate. He was staring up at us and pointed toward my broadcast partner. Once he got his attention, he spread his legs wide and pointed at his feet, lifting each one up very slowly as if he were marching in quicksand. Luckily for us he was smiling, after apparently being tipped off about the on-air joke regarding his lack of speed.

Some team officials also have a habit of getting bent out of shape over innocuous comments. I recall one day being inside a team office and hearing the General Manager's wife say "Someone really needs to talk to that wise guy radio man." She wasn't pleased with something he had said.

I recall the time we commented on-air something about the dusty, gravel parking lot at the ballpark that night. As we went to our next commercial break, the parking lot supervisor was standing right behind us, ready to let us know he wasn't thrilled with the comments. Some people just take themselves too seriously.

I was broadcasting another game one year in April and the General Manager came into the booth mid-broadcast to tell me I should never say how cold it is. (Temps were in the mid-30's that night and I had said so) I replied that my job was to inform the listener and make them feel as if they were right at the ballpark with me. I felt my listeners were smart enough to know how cold it was and wouldn't stay away from the park simply on account of me telling them it was freezing. He wanted a team shill while I viewed myself as a journalist.

One year I became familiar with the team's star pitcher. We sometimes ate together and talked often on road trips. I knew his wife a little, and I enjoyed hanging out with them both. Like many players, his family enjoyed listening to my live game broadcasts over the internet from his home on the West Coast. Knowing how my broadcasts were full of entertaining and enlightening tidbits about the team, he pulled me aside one day for a request.

"Do me a favor," he asked. "Don't mention that I'm married, ok? Nobody knows back home, and I want to keep it that way." I never mentioned him being married.

Perhaps my most memorable example of a broadcaster's inability to please everyone came one year as my broadcast partner and I were in the middle of our postgame show. As we continued our live broadcast, a large man walked up to our broadcast window and just stood there. We looked at him and he began saying something, but we were on the air and, thus, couldn't respond. When we signed off and removed our headsets, he was still there.

"I wasn't happy with the broadcast," he said with complete seriousness, as if he were our direct boss. The man was a part-time medic, part of the stadium's game-day staff. He then mumbled some bizarre, trivial complaint about something I cannot even remember. However, it just struck us as quite unusual that he felt he had to come to us with some kind of complaint about the broadcast.

A couple years later, my broadcaster phoned to tell me he had seen that same guy hitchhiking on the side of the road in a nearby town.

"Did you pick him up?" I asked.

"Nope," he replied. "He's just not happy with the broadcast."

-Rick Schultz

Father Versus Son

In 2010, while with the LumberKings, I witnessed the rarity of a father and son managing against one another. John Tamargo, Sr., manager of our club took on his son, Lansing Lugnuts' hitting coach and acting manager John Tamargo, Jr. We knew well in advance of the season that the two would meet in the July series, but it was only once we arrived in Lansing, it was confirmed that the younger JT would be stepping in to manage as regular skipper Sal Fasano was on vacation.

The game turned out to be one of the bigger barnburners of the season. Our veteran catcher, Blake Ochoa, went 2-for-3 with two home runs and a career-high seven RBI, but the LumberKings still fell, 12-7. Ochoa could have easily had 10 RBI, but his second-inning bases-loaded liner was caught by the diving centerfielder Kenny Wilson, turning it into a sacrifice fly.

The game would be the only match-up of the Tamargos, both of whom I interviewed for the pregame show the next day, as Fasano returned to his managerial duties the next evening. Still, given the rarity of a father-son managerial battle (possibly the first of its kind, I was never able to find another instance) and Ochoa's monster offensive night made it a game I'll never forget.

- Dave Lezotte

Don't Lose Your Head

The Hudson Valley Renegades began play in the New York-Penn League in 1994. The team became an instant hit, with nightly sellouts and a community bond that remains second-to-none. One of the prime attractions for kids at Renegades' games is the team's mascot, Rookie Renegade. The energetic and playful raccoon has been a staple at Dutchess Stadium since day one. Renegade games are quite a show, and for many Rookie is the main attraction.

Rookie's was quite pleased in 1997 when the organization presented him with a wife, Rene. The ballpark wedding was a grand affair. Following baseball tradition, the players formed two lines and touched their bats in the air, forming a tunnel. Through the improvised tunnel walked Rookie and his new wife, Rene.

One year later, Rookie and Rene were celebrating their first wedding anniversary at Dutchess Stadium. The Renegades organization had really become masters at creating fun, unique events for families to remember. In minor league baseball, the game is often secondary to the fun events, contests music and games played around the actual ballgame.

I recall Rookie was really flying high that night, as my broadcast partner and I watched him from our broadcast booth between innings. He pranced along the top of the third base dugout, imploring the crowd to cheer. He raced ten quick feet to the left, to a rousing applause. Then ten feet back the other way, to another round of cheers. Rookie was really on top of his game. Again, he gesticulated to the crowd and took off toward the far end of the dugout, and.....where did he go? Rookie was so caught up in the excitement of the moment that he zipped right off the end of the dugout. "There he goes!" we said with a laugh on the air.

As play resumed, a few pitches went by and we realized we hadn't seen Rookie pop back up onto the third base dugout. He's just waiting for the right moment, I thought. Or I imagined the cunning raccoon would sneak around to the other side with some trick up his sleeve. After one batter, still no raccoon. By that time, we saw some commotion over near the end of the dugout, and Bill and I began to ask each other, on the air, what may be going on.

"It looks like Rookie is still down there somewhere, having fun with the fans," I said. A few moments later, the umpire called time out as the team trainers and medical staff jogged over near the dugout.

At this point, we began to question whether the Renegades were starting to take this mascot theme a little too far. Clearly they were letting the "show" get in the way of the game. Both teams stood still on the field, as even more medical personnel arrived near the dugout.

"This is getting a little out of hand," I said. "To have fun is one thing. To let the make-believe mascot games affect the real game is another altogether." Amazingly enough, the right field gates opened and an ambulance began the slow drive down the first base line, around home plate, and over to the third base dugout.

The Renegades were always on the cutting edge, pushing the envelope to create a memorable evening for the family, but we commented that this stunt was a step too far since it was clearly intruding on the game.

After a 15-minute delay, the medics secured Rookie to a stretcher and hoisted him into the back of the ambulance. What theater! Some of the medical staff were yanking on the raccoon mascot head, but Rookie wasn't allowing them to pull it off. With the back doors still open, the ambulance began the slow ride back around to the right field gates. All the while, Rookie waved and gave the "thumbs up" to the applauding crowd. Boy, these Renegades sure did know how to put on a show.

A short time later we received some news to our radio booth. Rookie didn't get hurt, but the guy "playing" Rookie actually did. The employee wearing the Rookie costume had slipped off the dugout and broken his arm. It wasn't a joke, skit or part of a show. It was real!

The guy inside the costume was actually hurt, and he refused to let the medics remove the Rookie mascot head during the whole ordeal for fear of being fired. Rule number one was "Never be seen out of costume!" Plus, he couldn't stomach the thought of taking off his mascot head and upsetting a ballpark full of kids!

The courageous mascot spent some time healing and returned to action after a 15-day stint on the disabled list.

-Rick Schultz

Baseball's Top Ambassador

When I was working with the San Bernardino club in the California League, I had the pleasure of meeting the legendary Tommy Lasorda on numerous occasions, as we were a Single-A club for the Dodgers. One such moment will forever be etched in my mind.

We had to play a home doubleheader in May of 1998 due to a rainout. I was in the manager's office prior to game one and Tommy was sitting down there as well. He was saying that the guys needed something good to eat between games and asked if anyone knew if there was a good chicken joint nearby. I mentioned that there was a Popeye's Chicken not too far away and I looked up the number.

Lasorda dials them up and proceeds to tell them who he is and that he needs this large order of chicken that will be picked up by the clubbie. Naturally, the Popeye's manager was skeptical that it was truly Lasorda that was on the other end of the phone, so he asks for the phone number so that he can call back to confirm this isn't a hoax.

Once the manager calls back and is relatively certain that it is THE Tommy Lasorda, the former Dodgers manager proceeds to tell the manager that he wants them to donate the chicken for free. Tommy said in exchange he'd come down to the store personally to pick up the chicken and he'd go on air during our broadcast to promote the location.

True to his word, Lasorda accompanied the team clubbie, Peter Thompson, to pick up the chicken. According to what I was told by Peter, everyone's jaw hit the floor when they saw Tommy walk into the restaurant. In typical Lasorda fashion, he worked his way around the store, shaking hands with patrons and chatting with people. He even went behind the counter to help them box the chicken.

During game two of the doubleheader, Lasorda walks into my booth with a plate full of food, grabs a headset, sits down next to me, and takes a piece of paper out of his pocket that had the names of the Popeye's manager and employees written on it. He talked about how gracious they were to provide the chicken for the players and he mentioned everyone's name. If you didn't know better, you would have thought that he knew these people forever and wasn't just reading names off a sheet of paper.

As a postscript, that particular incident was 99% responsible for helping the team get a sponsorship from Popeye's the following season. Talk about great PR.

-Mike Saeger

Over The Bridge

Broadcasters do the zaniest things to pass time while on the road. Most broadcasters head to the ballpark around mid-afternoon for a night game, which leaves them all day to kill time in an unfamiliar town. This idle time in strange surroundings can lead to a variety of activities. Exercise and TV are two popular options to pass time, but they are certainly not the only things broadcasters do on the road.

For example, one former broadcast partner of mine used to pride himself on being able to walk from the team hotel to every ballpark in the league. This included the nine-mile walk in Williamsport, PA from the hotel to historic Bowman field. Or the long walk in Oneonta, NY where he tripped over a railroad bridge, landed in a tumbleweed and had to get stitches on a gaping hand wound. Then there was the time in Burlington, VT where he ended up practically part of a downtown pride parade.

In Jamestown, NY broadcasters could tour the dainty Lucille Ball museum. In Oneonta, NY they can trek to the Baseball Hall of Fame in Cooperstown. In Utica, there is the nearby casino. In the Hudson Valley you could take a 20 minute trip to West Point. Batavia's hotel is down the street from a dog racing track, and a seafood restaurant frequented by former Buffalo Bills quarterback Jim Kelly.

During the season I would often I would encounter visiting broadcasters and discuss what we'd do during the day before night games on the road. One dynamic duo confessed to having "spitting contests". They found a small bridge near Wahconah Park in Pittsfield, MA and had contests to see who could expectorate the farthest out into the stream 20 feet below. Who said baseball broadcasters were a childish bunch!

-Rick Schultz

Sleepless in September

When it comes to the post season undoubtedly October is the month that every team hopes to play in. For those who are at the minor league level it is September when championships are won and lost. The Amarillo Dillas of the Texas-Louisiana League were in the playoffs yet again and for a nine day stretch you never knew where they would wake up.

The final game of the regular season concluded shortly before Midnight on Saturday September 4th with a 14-3, rain delayed home win over the Lafayette Bullfrogs. Their first round opponent would be the Rio Grande Valley Whitewings, a team located at the bottom of the state of Texas. Amarillo is in the panhandle. After a night's sleep in their own beds the Dillas would travel by bus at midnight on Sunday as it is a 14+ hour bus trip to the Valley. We encountered some heavy rain and lightning during the 2nd half of the ride, so instead arriving around 3pm, we didn't check into the Best Western Harlingen until closer to 6pm on Monday. I can tell you first hand that while we were happy to be in a hotel, the rain and lighting that night did not allow for a restful evening.

Mother Nature wasn't kind for a good portion of Tuesday as the scheduled playoff game of 7:05 was delayed until 8:49pm. While the Dillas 7-2 win in this 2 out of 3 series was somewhat comforting, the journey was just beginning. When a game ends at 11:42pm a team with a 14-15 hour trip ahead of them is not going to have a lot of fun. By the time we left the stadium and found a fast food joint that was willing to serve 21 rather hungry individuals it was 2AM on Wednesday when we were headed north. Tired, cranky, restless, anxious are all words to describe the Dillas on this ride home, one that didn't culminate until 530pm….for a 7:05 start time. The Whitewings arrived after us so the start time was pushed back until 7:15, lol. As one might expect between two tired teams, it was a long one. Dillas survived despite making four errors 7-6 in 13 innings and 4:22.

Wednesday night was a day of rest for Amarillo but the travel would continue with a midnight Thursday departure. This time destination Alexandria, Louisiana where the Dillas would face the Aces in the title series for the third year in a row. No travel problems and smooth sailing as we checked into the" no name budget suites" before noon on Friday September 10th. An extra innings win that night coupled with another one on Saturday made the bus ride home much easier to deal with. It was an off day on Sunday the 12th and the team (and myself) slept in their own apartments.

If you are counting that is nine straight nights that the 1999 Amarillo Dillas slept in a different place than the previous night. I guess it wasn't too bad as on Monday the 13th, they claimed their first ever League championship. With a 13-4 win.

-Brett Quintyne

Best G.M. In The Game

You never know who you'll meet and become friendly with in minor league baseball. After a few years in the game, I had built a decent rolodex of contacts throughout the country. As the years go by, a broadcaster begins to build relationships with players, coaches, front office personnel, parent-club instructors, other broadcasters, etc. These relationships can be very gratifying and provide all kinds of great information about the inner workings of professional baseball.

One day in the summer of 2000, while preparing to broadcast a Norwich Navigator's game at Dodd Stadium in Connecticut, I saw a familiar face in the stands. As the Navigators took batting practice, I strolled down and said hello to my friend. We hadn't seen each other in a few years, and he was now working in player development for another major league club. We spent some time catching up and agreed to meet for a burger later that night.

After the game, we met at the local watering hole and shared stories from the past few years. We shared tales about each other's family and the many other mutual friends we had in the game. It got later and we headed toward the parking lot. As we approached the cars, I asked him a question about a particular major league superstar. His eyes lit up, and he then told me some great stories about this, and many other, players. We stood there talking for at least two hours! The topics evolved and we began talking about front office personnel. I asked him something about major league general managers, and he said Brian Cashman of the New York Yankees was absolutely the most thorough and prepared general manager he had ever encountered. He couldn't sing Cashman's praises enough. Pretty cool information for me to know being that I was broadcasting for the Yankees AA affiliate.

A couple years later I was hosting a daily sports-talk radio program on an ESPN Radio affiliate in Poughkeepsie, New York. We regularly had big-time guests on the program, and one day during the baseball season we were able to land Brian Cashman. On the air, I told him how my friend in player development had said he was a tremendous General Manager, unequivocally the best in the game. He was flattered and appreciated the kind words. For me, it proved you never know who you'll have a chance to meet and share stories with in minor league baseball.

-Rick Schultz

Tucson to Denver to Edmonton

In 2004, the Stingers had just completed a series in Tucson and were headed to Edmonton to face the Trappers. The team was scheduled on a flight from Tucson to Denver, change planes and then go from Denver to Edmonton. The first leg of the trip went without a hitch. That was not the case on the second part of our journey to the north. We get 30 minutes outside of Edmonton, the pilot comes on the intercom system, says, "Well, we've run into a little difficulty. Our windshield has just cracked like a jigsaw puzzle, and even though we're just 30 minutes outside Edmonton, we're going to divert the plane to of all places, Salt Lake City."

So we land in SLC at 2:30 p.m. and our new plane is supposed to be ready at 4:30 p.m. The team and the other passengers finally get the plane, but until 5:45. After we board the plane and are about ready to push off, the door opens to the plane, and the pilot comes on the intercom again and says, "Well, the grounds crew has decided it needs to clean out the bathroom tank." So that delays us even more. We finally take off at 6:30 p.m., and we land at Edmonton around 8:15 p.m. or so.

Now, normally they would have just postponed the game, but this is June 30th. July 1st is Canada Day, so June 30th was always sold out with a fireworks show after the game. So their general manager is negotiating with then Stingers manager Mike Brumley, we get a police escort through downtown Edmonton, which is about a 20-mile ride, and they finally negotiate that . . . we start at 9:50 p.m., but we have an 11 o'clock curfew. So we played four innings and then they suspended the game so they could start the fireworks on time at 11. And of course our personal bags didn't make it on the flight. Eventually, I got a knock on my door at 2 a.m. and finally got my bag.

-Steve Klauke

The No-Hitter I Never Saw

It was August 5, 2008, the anniversary of Harold Arlin's inaugural KDKA broadcast. I was working for the Windy City ThunderBolts, based in Crestwood, IL, on a purely internet-streamed broadcast with Nick Kovatch. The team in town that day was the Midwest Sliders, a road team in the independent Frontier League without its own broadcaster.

A wicked thunderstorm in the Chicago area had knocked out nearly all internet access everywhere in Standard Bank Stadium with the exception of the front office area. Each of the different tactics we tried to get the game on the air failed. It soon became clear that if we were going to have a broadcast that night, it had to somehow be from the office, which meant a game re-creation in the tradition of the broadcasting pioneers.

We collected a pair of mini-bats from the team's souvenir shop, a glove and a baseball, and set up shop at the desk next to the box office. A crew of front office interns alternated outside the front office, watching the game and messaging us the results of each pitch, which we faithfully re-created while cracking the mini-bats together or slamming the ball into the glove. Our pace placed us comfortable two or three batters behind the actual action, so as not to leave us needing to stall before the next update arrived in.

The ThunderBolts broke the game open early with a pair of huge rallies and the score was 13-0 heading into the ninth. As far as we knew, Midwest had managed only a solitary base hit against Windy City left-hander Isaac Hess, a seventh inning single. With one out in the ninth inning, however, we received word that the scoring had been changed from a hit to an error – at the very same time our co-workers came flooding jubilantly back into the office. Then we understood what had happened outside, though we still had to make our way through the final two at-bats in order to get there.

It was the first no-hitter in four years, to the day, in the Frontier League. More important, it was the first no-hitter in the 14-year history of the ThunderBolts' franchise.

It remains the only no-hitter I've ever called, and I never saw a pitch of it.

-Jesse Goldberg-Strassler

Taking Care Of Business

The more one is around baseball, the more wacky stories you come across. In 1999 I sat down for a pregame radio interview with one of the game's real good guys, future Florida Marlins manager Edwin Rodriguez. I asked Edwin what was the funniest moment he had ever seen in baseball. This was his response.......

"Back in Puerto Rico we were playing in front of 10,000 people. It was the 8th inning; I remember it like it was today. Everybody was on the field except the second baseman. Everybody was just waiting for the second baseman to come out to the field. So about five minutes later the second baseman came out, and he was ready. He was sprinting to second base, and he's got toilet paper hanging from his back! *In front of 10,000 people!* You can imagine, everybody was laughing and he didn't know what was going on. Finally, the shortstop said, "Listen, turn around. I'm gonna help you out a bit here." That was the funniest moment that I've had in baseball."

-Rick Schultz

Strike Three!

In my first season in Minor League Baseball, I decided to take a road trip to the California-Carolina League All Star Game, since I had never been, and figured that as part of a Professional team's staff, it might be an interesting experience.

The night before the game I ended up as the designated driver for another staff member from my club, a marketing executive for a rival team, a California league All Star (he was a pitcher), and his "girlfriend". Needless to say, I was hoping to find other people to talk to once we got to the bar. It was there I happened upon 4 guys at a square table covered corner to corner in empty beer bottles. There had to be at least 50 empty bottles, somewhere between 10 to 15 in front of each of the gentlemen.

Sure enough, I had found the umps. To be honest, they didn't seem all that intoxicated, which led me to believe that not only did they have an exceptional tolerance for alcohol, they'd probably been at that bar for about half a day. In any case, after sitting down and learning a few of the nuances of the MLB rulebook, one of the umps put $10 down that he would make a ridiculous punchout on a check-swing the next day (in the All Star game). He knew he was going to be the first base ump, so he figured at some point he'd get an appeal, and regardless of the situation, he was going to bring down the hammer.

I thought he was joking, but sure enough, in the 4th inning he got his appeal, and let loose one of the most ferocious crow-hop, Tiger Woods-esque arm swings I've ever seen. I yanked out my binoculars, and sure enough, he was grinning behind his gum-chewing, and I can only assume the others paid him his money.

- Dan Besbris

Is This Thing On?

Terry Kennedy had a fine major league career as a solid catcher for the Cardinals, Padres, Orioles and Giants. The 14-year big leaguer was a four-time All Star, hitting 113 home runs and driving in 628 runs. On a summer night in 1994 his career intersected with that of a well-known minor league Public Address announcer.

Kennedy was the skipper of the Vermont Expos, who were playing against the Hudson Valley Renegades at Dutchess Stadium in Fishkill, New York. During the Expos tough 3-1 loss at the hands of the Renegades, the Expos skipper came out to the mound to make a pitching change and pull pitcher Brady Frost. Now keep in mind that much of Dutchess Stadium, in its inaugural season, hadn't even been completed yet. The "press box" was a long, dusty room with framing set for individual broadcast booths. The largest "booth" was shared by the Public Address announcer, official scorer and scoreboard operators. The Public Address system consisted of a microphone with a switch that you had to switch to "On" in order to be heard.

As the pitching change was being made, some guests were talking in the back of the booth and didn't notice the P.A. mic falling to the floor and toggling the switch to "On". One guest in the booth cracked that the pitcher "couldn't even break the speed limit on Route 84," which sits out past the right field wall. Renegades P.A. man Rick Zolzer responded,

"This guy couldn't win the women's division in the speed pitch challenge!" Zolzer, a ballplayer himself, made the joke to his friends, not intending for it to go any further. While most of the players and fans didn't even hear the comment, Kennedy heard it all out on the pitching mound.

When the game ended, as most of the media members and technical crew were packing up, Terry Kennedy came charging up the steps toward the press box. He barreled toward "The Zolz," reaching through the unfinished press box window as he screamed and yelled. Still in uniform, he was practically foaming at the mouth with anger. With many still milling around on the press box level, the 6'3" manager made his point loud and clear. It was very loud and very clear that none of his players should be treated that way.

After a short, heated back and forth with Zolzer , Kennedy turned and exited the stadium's press level. The uniformed manager bounded down the steps to the main concourse, where he was greeted by a flock of fans. Kennedy spent the next ten minutes signing autographs and chatting it up with the Hudson Valley faithful.

Later that night, Rick Zolzer phoned Terry Kennedy at the team hotel. While not being above a good wise crack, he insisted that he would never intentionally demean a professional ballplayer. Kennedy said he was shocked to hear the wise crack from Zolzer, who a few years later would become the Public Address Voice of the New Jersey Nets. The two men had a cordial conversation, and a short while later the manager and team received a delivery of pizza and beer, courtesy of Rick Zolzer.

The next morning, Terry Kennedy appeared as a guest of Zolzer on a local radio program, and the two again shared some jokes about the entire incident. During the first inning of that night's game, Renegade mascots Rookie and Rene even delivered roses to Kennedy in the third base coach's box. The two men even hung out for a while before a game later that season when Hudson Valley was in Vermont to play the Expos. The inauspicious comment over the loudspeaker actually turned out to be the beginning of a unique minor league friendship.

-Rick Schultz

Double Comeback Hysteria

I've broadcast 327 games in nearly three years with the Charleston RiverDogs.

I've seen my fair share of humorous, odd, thought-provoking, head-scratching moments. I've seen the same pitcher walk 10 batters in one outing, 8 in another, and allow 5 runs in 3 innings without giving up a single hit. I've seen a bullpen combine to throw 14 straight balls before a suspect swing on number 15 resulted in a foul ball to halt the streak of futility. I've seen the opposing team commit 6 errors….IN ONE INNING!! I've seen two no-hitters last all the way to the 9th inning only to lose them and then get no-hit less than a week after the second occurrence. I've seen a four-K inning twice in the same year. I've seen the sprinkler system get set off TWICE at the same ballpark during two different games (one was in 11th inning of a tie game, nonetheless). I've seen three power outages in the same year…I usually think of ballparks as safe places!! Still, there are others that stick out and always will stick out.

August 25 & 29, 2009 became dates that not only represented two of the many walkoff wins that I've witnessed but also THE two most dramatic come-from-behind victories I can recall.

August 25 was the first of a four-game set against the Rome Braves at Joseph P. Riley, Jr. Park in Charleston. The RiverDogs were 10-6 against the Braves to that point in '09 and an impressive 6-1 at The Joe. However, the evening started with a bang for Rome, scoring in its first five at-bats for a monstrous 9-1 lead in taking what looked like complete control. I honestly expected the game to spiral completely out of reason. Granted 9-1 wasn't a particularly good feeling with still four innings left to play. I became more preoccupied with the difficult task of writing a painful post-game recap and later on catching some late night TV. Our offense thought otherwise.

The bottom of the 5th started with three straight hits, which included a RBI double by catcher Jeff Farnham, who had been added to the roster less than month before and would go on to collect four hits in his next four at-bats. Not bad for a 27th round pick who wasn't even supposed to sign. After a strikeout put one man down, back-to-back RBI knocks from Abraham Almonte and Corban Joseph completed the first four-run inning for a 9-5 count entering the sixth (Almonte finished with three hits to up his hitting streak to a career-best 16 games…it would end at 26 games for the second-longest streak in team history. Joseph joined Farnham in the four-hit club after only going 2-for-24 against Rome before this night). Don't forget…I did say it was the *first* four-run inning.

Zero's graced the scoreboard in the sixth and the Riley Park crowd sang "Take Me Out to the Ballgame" before the bottom half of the seventh following another Rome goose egg. Earlier in the year, the RiverDogs erased a four-run deficit…after the 7th inning stretch…beating Rome 7-6 in a walkoff triumph. This bottom half had a decent script at the outset: Melky Mesa stroked a RBI single trimming the deficit to three runs at 9-6, but with two outs and two strikes on Garrison Lassiter, the inning was nearly done…this wouldn't be much of a story if it ended here. Lassiter worked a walk to put two on and two down for Neall French. French was a burly 26-year-old catcher/first baseman/DH just signed by the Yankees before the season. Otherwise, he would've suited up for the Florence Freedom of the independent Frontier League. He's one of the nicest players I've had the chance to meet, fully embodying the "speak softly and carry a big stick" philosophy once famously uttered by Teddy Roosevelt. My, my, my, did that come into play in this instance.

French worked a full count, fouling off several pitches in the process. Then on the next offering, with the runners going, and down by 3, French connected on a belt-high pitch. It was so loud but I could barely hear it. It kept carrying until the left-centerfield wall couldn't contain it anymore…I've never heard a crowd erupt like that. The game was tied at 9-9 and there was no doubt the Dogs were going to complete this epic. It didn't come in regulation, though. That had to wait until the 12th inning.

Farnham walked to start the frame and with one out, Jose Pirela blistered a line-drive to centerfield that carried right over the head of Calvin Culver and all the way to the wall. Farnham unhooked the caboose and scored without a throw for a 10-9 final and immediate bedlam. I thought I was pretty lucky. No, very lucky. Some guys never get to see a comeback like that. I only had to wait four days to see it happen again…in the same homestand.

On August 29, the RiverDogs were scheduled to take on the Augusta GreenJackets in a doubleheader. The only reason for the doubleheader was because of a torrential downpour in the Charleston area the night before. Knowing what I do now, I was pretty thankful for that storm.

Game one wasn't the second epic comeback in question…we'll get to that later…game one, though, had its own flare for the dramatic. According to South Atlantic League rules, any scheduled doubleheader will feature two, seven-inning games. That would prove to be particularly impactful in this tale. Augusta snatched a 2-0 lead in the 4th, but Charleston scored 2 in the 5th and pushed the go-ahead run across in the 6th, a RBI single by Farnham…what a shocker. The lead was 3-2 in the top of the seventh with Augusta runners on 1st and 2nd with two outs. Number 3 batter Josh Mazzola looped a single to right-field to set up this unreal spot. The Charleston right-fielder was Almonte, who not only hit the game-tying RBI single in the fifth but was making just his 7th start of the year in RF. He collected the ball on a hop. The tying runner at second for Augusta was Johnny Monell, the usual starting catcher, but because of the doubleheader, he pinch hit to start the inning for a much faster runner. Fortunately for Almonte, the lack of speed worked in his favor. A perfect throw hit Farnham's glove in more than enough time to apply the game-ending tag for the 3-2 win and the game one victory. Now, we can talk about the second eight-run comeback in less than 100 hours.

In that game two, I saw an Augusta team ratchet 11 hits in four innings en route to an 8-0 lead (It took them 7 innings to get 8 hits in game one, mind you.) I remember saying several times on the broadcast that the R'Dogs had just made a monumental eight-run comeback four days before against Rome and that it certainly wasn't out of the realm of possibility. But, could it really happen again, that soon after the biggest comeback in history of Riley Park?

I started to get my answer in the bottom of the sixth. Two of the first three batters were retired, but the next seven batters got on base – five hits and two walks – plating six runs to cut the score to 8-6. Corban Joseph nearly tied the game on the next pitch, but first-baseman Mazzola made an incredible diving stop to take away at least a double and preserve the *momentary* two-run cushion. In the bottom of the seventh (remember this was the last inning due to the funky rule), I sat up in my chair running so many different scenarios through my head. This inning could've ended so many different ways…1-2-3, a couple hits with three straight K's, a double-play with a popout and no one would've ever remembered an 8-6 South Atlantic League final score in late August. You'll like this ending.

Garrison Lassiter hit a two-out opposite-field RBI double moving the score to 8-7 and was then lifted from the game for pinch-runner Ray Kruml, a usual starter and one of the fastest players in the league. Gosh, I love plot twists. The R'Dogs next better was catcher Mitch Abeita, who contributed a RBI single the inning before. Abeita proceeded to hit what looked like an ordinary groundball deep in the hole at shortstop. Augusta's SS was Ehire Adrianza, a guy who had not only spent time on the Giants' 40-man roster but was one of the best defensive shortstops in the circuit. Adrianza was able to barely get a glove tip on the horsehide to slow its progress. Kruml had darted for third on contact, then inexplicably shot home to try and tie the game. Adrianza had more than enough time to throw home to catcher Monell for the final out and end the game…but he didn't take that time. Instead, he bobbled the ball once he slowed it and rushed an off-balance throw to the plate which bounced wide and to the first-base side permitting Kruml to score and set the crowd in another frenzy….8-8…again, the game would go to extras to send the faithful home with a smile.

Three and a half scoreless innings led to the bottom of the 11th, where Charleston's Taylor Grote rolled a single to right field to leadoff, moved to second on an errant pickoff throw and scored the game-winner on Addison Maruszak's RBI single to right-centerfield alley. A 9-8 final, another raucous RiverDogs walkoff and two of my finer moments in the booth at The Joe.

Granted the actual calls are *slightly* distorted (I have a tendency to get quite animated), but hey, when you see something that you've never seen before, natural forces take over. Kind of like what happened to our players on those two nights. They may have had comebacks with more runs in a different city with more family present...anything could've happened. However, I'd be willing to stake plenty on the fact that these two instances will be filed in a special vault for those considered. I know they will never be far from my mind.

- Danny Reed

Snakes

Doug Greenwald has endured many a bus trip during his minor league broadcasting career, but reptiles remind him of one July trip in particular. During his Texas-Louisiana days, the team was taking a 10-hour overnight bus trip from Lafayette, LA to Lubbock, TX. In the middle of their journey, the bus broke down in the middle of the Texas desert.

As many of the players slept, the bus came to a stop on the side of desolate I-20. They were without food, beverages or air conditioning, and quite a ways from the next rest stop. As night turned into day, the sun beat down. As the hours began to pass, some players climbed through the crawl hole onto the top of the bus, which – even in the blazing sun – was cooler than the stuffiness inside. Some tried to catch some sleep on top of the bus.

While some players strolled away from the bus to take care of business, a predominance of snakes in the desert dissuaded many of them from going too far. This fear of reptiles kept Doug close to the bus. Upon picking up on Greenwald's ophidiophobia, one of the players came back to the bus and surprised him with a huge snakeskin. Exactly what he must have wanted to see on very little sleep in the hot desert!

After almost four hours, another bus arrived to take the team on to their destination. They completely emptied all of their belongings from the original bus and loaded them onto the new one, minus the snakeskin. After a long, hot day in the sun, the team arrived in Lubbock, TX at 5pm. With little rest, they managed to win the game 14-8.

-Doug Greenwald

One Day I'll Be Out There

Minor League ballplayers don't get many days off. Most weeks the team will play six or seven games, so off-days are few and far between. So when players have an off-day, they usually want to make the most of it.

The Hudson Valley Renegades in the New York-Penn League would usually get three days off per season. On most off-days, groups of players would often take the 90-minute trip from Fishkill, New York down to Manhattan so the guys from across the country could experience New York City for the first time.

One of the great things about minor league baseball, from a broadcaster's perspective, is the friendships you can establish with the players. In doing so, you are able to witness some of the most amazing and meaningful moments. During an off day in 1996 I was fortunate to take a trip down to Yankee Stadium with many Renegade players to see the Yankees play the Seattle Mariners.

On this summer night, we sat halfway up the upper deck, directly behind home plate. With sparse attendance, there weren't many fans sitting directly around us. Renegades outfielder Craig Monroe, from Texarkana, Texas, peered out to the glistening green grass, clearly struck by the beauty of this historic ballpark. He was only 19, yet he looked back from his seat and said, "Someday that'll be me."

An inning later, Ken Griffey Jr. raced in and made an astounding, diving catch to rob a base hit. Monroe was still in awe of everything – Griffey, the ballpark and his chances of someday being out there in this beautiful yard. "I'm gonna be out there someday," he said.

Five years later, Craig Monroe made it to the big leagues with the Texas Rangers. On July 31 of that year the Rangers played in New York at Yankee Stadium. Craig Monroe played right field and went 1 for 3 with a run scored. A dream had come true as Craig Monroe was out on that same Yankee Stadium field, playing in a major league ballgame.

As of 2016, Craig Monroe has concluded his playing career and is now a highly-acclaimed studio analyst for the Detroit Tigers.

-Rick Schultz

Princeton Picasso

Princeton, West Virginia, population 7,652, is the smallest town to host an affiliated minor league baseball team. It also hosted the longest game I've been fortunate to call. My club, the Burlington Royals, was playing its final road trip of the season. The game was nothing to write home about through 9 innings -- which surely added to the collective angst shared by those on the field, in the stands and in the press box. Safe to say, it was a game people were just hoping would end.

In the bottom of the 11th, Princeton -- the Devil Rays affiliate -- had runners at first and second with no outs. Royals manager Darryl Kennedy went out to the mound and decided to have his pitcher, Ted Gjeldum, walk Princeton's number seven hitter to load the bases with nobody out. (I found out later Gjeldum said, "Let's do it!" when told of the decision) Sure enough, Gjeldum struck out the number eight hitter. Then came the panic move - with one out and the bases loaded, Princeton manager Jamie Nelson tried a suicide squeeze. The result: the batter popped up the bunt, catcher Nick Doscher made the grab, then threw to third for the force to end the inning. It was clear then, this game had no end.

Nelson was later ejected in the 16th (his pitching coach had been tossed all the way back in the fourth inning). Both teams scored two runs in the 16th, before the Royals tallied one more in the 17th. Princeton had the tying run at second base with two outs, but Jose Diaz retired Dustin Biell on a ground out to end the ballgame. I swear first baseman Jake Lane almost dropped the throw over on the final play!

It took four hours and fifty three minutes, before 814 fans, two teams, a giddy press box and official scorer Bob Redd. Baseball isn't always a work of art, and it wasn't a Picasso on this night, but it provided great theater in a small town in West Virginia.

-Ed Cohen

Strange Night At The Park

The strangest game I've ever called took place on August 27th, at the tail end of the 2009 regular season. I was working for the Lakewood (NJ) BlueClaws and we were in Hagerstown (MD) to finish a three-game series with the Suns. The entire night wasn't as much one wacky event as a series of things that added up to one odd night at the ballpark.

It all started with BlueClaws manager Dusty Wathan's plan to give his shortstop, Troy Hanzawa, who had played in all but eight games to that point, a day off. The BlueClaws had already qualified for the post-season and he wanted to rest some guys. No problem, right? As the second batter of the game, second baseman Harold Garcia strikes out on a check swing, only he thought he held up. He argued, was ejected, and, as the only other middle infielder on the roster, that was the end of Troy Hanzawa's day off.

In the top of the third, with the BlueClaws already leading 5-1, BlueClaws right fielder Brian Gump flew into the ol' 8-4 fielder's choice. In the middle of the third, the lights went out. Ordinarily, this is not a big deal; you just turn them back on. Here, however, they wouldn't seem to go back on. The game was legitimately in jeopardy until they came back on 30 minutes later. Most of the fans, however, didn't seem to care. That meant 30 more minutes to take advantage of Thirsty Thursday and the accompanying $1 beers.

The BlueClaws had a 7-1 lead after four innings and did what they could to prolong the evening. They walked *TEN* Hagerstown hitters, though only allowed two runs. Reliever Jordan Ellis turned in what may be the most eclectic line of the season. In two innings of relief, one batter put the ball in play. He struck out five. But he hit two, walked three, and threw *FIVE* wild pitches.

On top of all that, one thing happened that night that I've never seen before, or since. BlueClaws OF Vladimir de los Santos came up to bat in the middle innings, stepped into the box, tapped the bat on the ground to get ready, called time, stepped out, and looked at the bat. It was broken. He went up to the plate with a broken bat, a great way to cap off a weird night in western Maryland.

- Greg Giombarrese

The Pillowcase Game

Many teams begin a bus trip with a great way to kill some time - the "Pillowcase Game". Otherwise known as the "Driver's License Game". The origins of this minor league staple are unknown, although the idea is simple. Someone comes to the front of the bus with an open pillowcase, and everyone tosses in a Driver's License. Players, coaches, broadcasters and whoever is on the bus. For each ID you throw in, you contribute $1 to the pot.

The ID's are then picked one by one – first out gets his money back, last one wins the pot. With about 30 people on the bus, the pot is often around $100. The game requires one person to hold the pillowcase and another, the Master of Ceremonies, to build anticipation and pick the ID's one by one. With each pick, players erupt with enthusiasm and targeted barbs directed toward the owner of the card. As the picks are made, the IDs are passed back through the bus to their owner. Adding to the drama are the raucous comments about ugly pictures, outdated hair, etc.

During one trip, a big first-baseman was picking the ID's. With each one he gave some pointed, good natured comments. "Oh man, that picture is horrible!," he said. "Did you just wake up?" Just then the bus swerved and – WHACK – he smacked his head on the luggage compartment. Now *that* made everyone on the bus crack up!

There is serious strategy to the Driver's License Game. Some players pool their cards together in hopes of splitting the winnings. Others stay with the single approach. While the ID's are being picked, some players try not to pay attention by putting headphones on or pretending to sleep. The game is also richly steeped in its ground rules, as this is serious business. The cardinal sin of the game is to call out another guy's luck by pointing out that he's still in the running to win the pot.

The game really gets fun after about a half hour when there are only a few cards remaining. The MC usually pulls them out to let the crowd know who are still remaining. The suspense builds as the final few are picked.

The 1997 Hudson Valley Renegades' first Pillowcase Game of the year was won by young phenom Matt White, who had just signed for a record bonus of $10,200,000. You can imagine the abuse he took for that one. (White was a great guy and, in fact, quite a generous teammate who often picked up tabs for team meals, etc.)

Another memorable Pillowcase finale involved Renegades boisterous outfielder Mike DeCelle. DeCelle was one of just two left in the pot, and he was taking a reverse psychological approach. "I don't want to win!" he yelled. "I don't want to win! Pick me! Pick me! Pick me!" They did pick him, and he lost.

Regardless of the outcome, the Pillowcase Game is a great way to loosen up and pass some windshield time. Winning and then splurging on a fancy lunch is also nice.

-Rick Schultz

View From The Seats

An idea I had throughout one season was to broadcast from the outfield seats, just like Harry Caray on WGN broadcasts at Wrigley Field.

On a Sunday afternoon, I decided to set up shop in one of the group deck areas in straight-away left field. It ended up being one of the warmest days of the entire summer, and with no cover it was definitely a day where sunscreen needed to be applied after nearly every inning. In retrospect, I underestimated how hot it would be. I would have picked a different day, but this was the only day left in the season where the group deck area was not occupied.

It was interesting and challenging to broadcast from the left field stands. It was certainly difficult to call balls and strikes and tough to determine where exactly the ball was traveling. Balls hit to center and right field looked exactly the same off the bat. The first play of the game was a popup to shortstop. Off the bat, I swear it looked like it would end up over my head!

Later in the game, I had a home run ball come about five feet away from me! The ball was hit by Kernels catcher Francis Larson and made for one of the more memorable home run calls of the season! It was still only the second most memorable souvenir I received on the season though! (See my story about the foul ball also in this book.)

-Morgan Hawk

Your Routine 5-3-2 Putout

It was a rainy evening in Harlingen, Texas where the Amarillo Dillas were playing game 1 of their playoff series against the Rio Grande Valley Whitewings on September 7th, 1999. Bad weather never assists in playing a clean game and in this instance four guys made what should have been a routine play a bizarre one.

Domingo Michel led off the bottom of the 5th inning with the Whitewings trailing the Dillas 5-1. Michel hit a ground ball to the third basemen Derek Henderson who fielded it cleanly. Due to the rain Michel had trouble getting out of the batters' box and fell down a step past home plate. Henderson had all the time in the world to throw to first but the wet ball caused an errant throw and it tailed towards the first base dugout. Michel now realizing he had a chance to reach safely began to run to first base. The first baseman Jared Mcalvain chased the ball as he should have but the oddity is that the catcher Shawn Hughes was sprinting up the first base line with the runner! Mcalvain made the play as he threw a strike to the moving target Hughes covering first base.

We've seen catchers backing up a play at first but making a putout at first is a rarity. The way to score that is 5-3-2.

-Brett Quintyne

Superman

One of the great things about Minor League Baseball is that fans can get so close to the action. To a child, these close settings can be magical – a chance to see their heroes in uniform up close. Oftentimes, they can meet their favorite player or get an autograph. Sometimes when fans are so close to the players, it can be as much of a thrill for the guys in uniform as it is for the fans. Such was the case on night at Pittsfield's cozy Wahconah Park.

Pittsfield's Wahconah Park was built in 1919, and has recently played host to independent, non-affiliated minor league teams. From 1989 to 2000, the park was home to the Pittsfield Mets of the New York-Penn League. Nestled in the Berkshire region of Massachusetts, the park has traditionally been home to a loyal, if smaller, home crowd. With wooden owls hanging from the roof of the grandstand to scare away birds and their birdie mess, Wahconah is full of character. (Interestingly, they occasionally have sun delays during games at Wahconah Park, because the park was laid out during an era that featured games solely during the day. At dusk, the sun sets behind left-center field and games are often halted because batters, fans and umpires cannot see the ball.)

One Saturday night in mid-1999, the Hudson Valley Renegades won a 3-1 game in 10 innings over the Mets at Wahconah. The most exciting thing to happen on this night, however, had nothing to do with the big win. Before the game, future major leaguer Jorge Cantu was warming up near the Renegades first base dugout when he spotted a familiar face in the nearby wooden grandstand. The 17-year old Cantu walked toward the stands and stretched out his hand. He was greeted cordially by area resident Christopher Reeve, who often took in a game at Wahconah Park.

"I was like 'Wow, what's he doing here," said Cantu. "I had the chance to shake Superman's hand!"

A few years later, Cantu would be playing in sold-out major league ballparks. Chances are, he still hasn't forgotten the night he got to meet Superman in Pittsfield, Massachusetts.

-Rick Schultz

Unlimited Possibilities

In 2007, the Rancho Cucamonga Quakes were playing in High Desert against the Mavericks. Stater Brothers Stadium was built in 1991 and has not had many improvements made to it since. It's in the middle of nowhere up Highway 15 on the way to Las Vegas. There is a sign a mile away from the ballpark as you enter the city of Adelanto that says, "The City with Unlimited Possibilities." You want to know why it says that, because there is literally nothing around but the ballpark and an industrial mill a couple miles away that is visible past the left center field wall. Unlimited possibilities....you betcha, nothing stopping you!

Regardless of the ballpark situation, our game was about to begin and for one reason or another, one of the two umpires scheduled for the game did not show up. Both teams were up in arms about the situation and neither wanted to play with just one umpire. So, our clubhouse attendant stepped up and was given the bases to officiate (no way would he have ever been behind the plate). He put any bias aside and did a pretty good job. He had umpired some high school games before and played in college, so he knew the game. Like I said, he did a fine job. There were no real close calls, his rotations were adequate and neither manager cared to argue anything.

The best part about our clubbie going out and umpiring wasn't just that he was doing it, but the fact that we was wearing sandals, athletic shorts and a t-shirt. He looked like Joe-Anybody climbing down from the stands. It was hilarious!

-Jeff Levering

The King

One of the hallmarks of minor league baseball is the unique array of in-stadium entertainment acts. Parks feature mascots, musicians, magicians and every zany thing in between. One of the best, and certainly most energetic, acts I've ever seen made an appearance at New Jersey's Skyland's Park in 1994.

As the Hudson Valley Renegades and New Jersey Cardinals battled it out during a mid-summer night in New Jersey, the crowd was treated to one of the most unique minor league acts out there – Elvis impersonator Frankie Capri. Not only did he look like The King of Rock and Roll, but he also tailored his act to fit the venue. Skyland's Park is about an hour outside of New York City, and I can recall Capri's Elvis rendition of Frank Sinatra's "New Jersey, New Jersey." Not only was Capri engaging, but it also seemed that he never took a break. As I recall the night, I remember him performing between almost every inning, including the pregame and postgame. Some fans cheered loudly for Franki Capri, while others jeered his bombastic, over-the-top performance.

The lasting memory I'll always have of Franki Capri that night was long after the game had concluded. We had wrapped up our postgame show and were diligently packing away the radio equipment. The park was, by now, inhabited by only a few cleaning crew members. As we peered out of our booth and onto the lower concourse behind home plate, Franki Capri was still performing! For nobody! The park was empty, yet he was giving it his all, complete with dancing gyrations....."New Jersey, New Jersey!" He was still dancing as we left the park, and for that I'll always remember Frankie Capri.

-Rick Schultz

Pre-Game Wedding

During my third season in Clinton, I participated in a unique baseball wedding. Our strength coach was determined to keep a family tradition alive, getting married on a specific day during the season.

His father, grandfather, great grandfather, etc. had all been married on the exact same August day, and that day happened to fall on a LumberKings' home game. Keeping with tradition, he held his wedding that afternoon before batting practice in the sprawling city park nestled between our stadium and the Mississippi River.

We all showed up to a fountain located in the park, just a few yards behind the left-field fence. The bride and groom were decked out in the usual gown and tux, but the rest of the wedding party was very casual, most players showing up in khakis and a polo shirt. Our Sunday baseball chaplain presided over the union, with our pitching coach and his wife serving as the Best Man and Maid of Honor. Players from the team and members of our office staff – myself included – rounded out the wedding party. I did my part by serving as the witness, signing the marriage license.

The wedding went off without a hitch, and everyone was invited up to the stadium's picnic pavilion for cupcakes as an informal wedding reception. After about an hour, everyone cleared out to get ready for stretch and batting practice and baseball life continued on as normal.

-Dave Lezotte

Costly Blunder

On April 19ᵗʰ, 1994 during the first home stand of the new Pacific Coast League team in Salt Lake City, the Buzz were trailing Albuquerque 5-1 in the third inning with the bases loaded and no outs. Bernardo Brito, who some called the "Dominican Crash Davis", hits a ball towards the alley in right-centerfield off Dukes' pitcher Ben Van Ryn that just clears the fence for a game-tying grand slam. But the runner at first, Paul Russo, thought the ball was caught and was headed back to first base. Brito passed him between first and second, which makes it an out and turns a grand slam into a three-run single.

So instead of tied 5-5, at the end of three it's 5-4. And you're thinking, well, its 5-4 at the end of three innings; it's a PCL game in one of the league's high altitude parks, so something else is going to happen, right. But nobody scored the rest of the way, so the final was Albuquerque 5, Salt Lake 4.

-Steve Klauke

Post-Game Hilarity

I landed my first professional baseball broadcasting gig by selling programs. When the Hudson Valley Renegades club relocated to Fishkill, NY, from Erie, PA, I immediately applied with the team. Luckily for me, I landed a job as one of a few game program salesmen at the park. I would show up early, stuff my programs with promotional goodies and head out to sell them as fast as I could. Once I got rid of my nightly lot – which was sometimes as early as the third inning – I would hustle up to the radio booth to help out team radiocaster Bill Rogan.

During those first couple seasons, I was in charge of conducting post-game interviews on the field immediately following the game. I would stand poised, ready for the game to end, at which time I would dart onto the field and grab the star of the game. I would tape a brief interview into my tape recorder, and we would play it during the post-game show, making it seems as if it were live. Over the years I had quite a few memorable interviews.

As an 18-year-old rookie in 1994, I began by writing up questions on an index card. That way I would have solid points to bring up during my interview. I gathered my questions and got ready to head down to the field during the ninth inning of a game that year, when Rogan called me back.

"Do you have your questions?" he asked.

"Sure I do." I responded.

"Can I see them?" he wondered. I handed them over, and he proceeded to tear the card into a hundred pieces.

"What the heck are you doing?" I shouted. "I need those! Those questions are for the interview!"

"You don't need them," Bill said calmly. "You watched the game. You broadcast the game. You saw it all. Just be natural and ask the questions. You don't need notes." Needless to say it was a choppy interview that night, but the first step toward becoming a much better professional interviewer.

Another interview that stands out is the one after Julian Redman smacked a bases-loaded, game winning hit in the bottom of the ninth inning to lead the Erie Seawolves to a win over the Hudson Valley Renegades. I raced onto the field, grabbed Redman, and began the interview......

"What were you thinking as you knocked in the game-winning run?" I asked.

"Um....well.....uh...." He struggled to spit out an answer. "Well....you know....I....I just......I just did what I could and we won the ballgame."

"Were you expecting the fastball?" I followed up.

"Um...uh....well....we won the game, big win, exciting win for us." He said hesitantly. After a few more questions we wrapped up the interview and I zipped up to the broadcast booth to play the interview over the air. As I arrived up to the booth, I told Bill I had a good interview with Julian Redman.

"Why did you interview Redman?" he asked quizzically.

"What do you mean, why?" I retorted with some attitude. "The game-winning hit." He turned to look directly at me.

"Redman didn't have the game winning hit," he stated. "Redman was on deck." My jaw dropped, and then the anger kicked in. I fired my notes at the wall in disgust.

"How could I make that mistake!" I yelled. For that, future major leaguer Julian Redman will always have a special place in my heart.

Perhaps the most "unique" interview I ever conducted – and undoubtedly the quickest – occurred on a September Sunday evening in Pittsfield, MA. It was the final week of the season, as the leaves began to turn and football was in the air. I was a huge Buffalo Bills fan, and Bill was a die-hard fan of the New York Giants. Coincidently, the Bills and Giants were playing this night on Sunday Night Football, which would begin at 8:00 p.m. Our game between the Renegades and Pittsfield Mets began in the late afternoon at Wahconah Park. We hoped for a quick game, so we could rush back to the hotel to watch my Bills beat his Giants.

Fortunately for us, Pittsfield won the quick game and we had less than an hour to complete our postgame show and get back to the hotel. Each portion of our postgame show was sponsored by a paying advertiser, so we had to conclude the broadcast as usual.

By this time in my career, I had developed a sense of pride around my stimulating, engaging post-game interviews. I cherished the five or ten minutes to chat with the star of the game. However, this night we were in a predicament, for each additional minute on the air was an additional minute of the football game we'd miss. We decided on a compromise. This was my complete interview.....

"It's time for our postgame interview," Bill said. "Now let's send it down to the field, where Rick Schultz is standing by with the star of the game."

"OK Bill," I began. "I'm down on the field with Pee Wee Lopez, who had the game winning hit for the Mets. Pee Wee, big win for your club."

"Thanks," Lopez responded. "It was a big hit and a big win for us."

"Alright," I quipped. "Thanks Pee Wee. And now I'll send it back up to Bill in the booth."

That was it. The complete interview lasted about ten seconds. And yes, we did make it back to the hotel for pizza and kickoff.

-Rick Schultz

Horsing Around

This one happened back in 1992 when I was working for the Augusta Pirates in South Atlantic League and might be the strangest brawl I've witnessed in more than 20 years in the business.

We were playing at Charleston, SC one night and facing former No. 1 draft pick Joey Hamilton. I don't recall all of the details in great clarity but I do remember that it all started with Augusta outfielder Marty Neff at the plate. Marty was a pretty decent hitter at that point in his career and would go on to hit 23 homeruns that season between Augusta and Salem. Hamilton, of course, would go on to pitch a number of years in the majors.

On this particular night, Neff was facing Hamilton. I don't recall anything happening earlier that would have flared tempers, so this may have been an isolated incident. Nonetheless, Neff hit a little dribbler up the first base side that was fielded by Hamilton. Joey applied the tag but Neff took umbrage at the forcefulness of the tag. The two had words and the next thing you know both dugouts emptied. Within mere moments we had a bit of a free-for-all taking place on the field.

Now this is nothing terribly unusual, except that they had mounted police officers at the ballpark. For whatever reason, the officers decided it was their duty to intercede. Besides the fact that that was something you almost never see in a fight, the melee frightened at least one of the horses on the field, who proceeded to stomp on the leg of one of the Charleston players who was on the ground.

I don't remember the name of the player, but according to reports the next day, the young man had a lingering forget-me-not from the previous night, as the horse had left a bruise in shape of a hoof-print on the leg of that player.

-Mike Saeger

You're Part of This Team

As mentioned earlier, my professional broadcasting career began in 1994. As an 18-year-old, I began by selling programs for the Hudson Valley Renegades. After meeting the team's number one broadcaster, I eventually weaseled my way into a part-time role on the team's radiocasts as well. I would sell my programs as fast as I could and then race up to the booth to help out on air and conduct post-game interviews. Even though I wasn't getting paid to be on the air, it was like a dream come true to work and travel with a professional baseball team.

Often, I packed a sleeping bag and slept on the floor in the main broadcaster's room in some dumpy hotel. There was nowhere in the world I wanted to be more than on that bus, heading from town to town across the New York Penn League. What baseball fan wouldn't want to travel with a pro team, calling minor league action!

Since I wasn't getting paid to do the games, I was also working overnights in a factory. For home games, I'd work the game at Dutchess Stadium, then head to my overnight job. On weekends, I'd hop on the team bus or drive in my own car, so I could be back in time for my factory job Monday night.

I recall our trip to Oneonta, New York to play the Oneonta Yankees that year. On day two of a two-game series, the team took a day trip to nearby Cooperstown, for a tour of the Baseball Hall of Fame. For this particular road trip, I worked my overnight shift and then headed to Oneonta in my own car. I arrived at the dumpy team motel in Oneonta as the team was boarding the bus. As I walked up to say hello to some of the guys, the team's manager, Doug Sisson, gave me a pat on the back.

"Are you coming with us to the Hall of Fame?" he said.

"Well, if I can," I said, surprised. I never expected to be invited.

"If you *can*," Sisson shot back. "You're part of this team, aren't you?" I proudly said yes, and boarded the bus. It was a day to remember at the Hall of Fame.

Six years later, in 2000, I had moved up the ladder to broadcast for the Yankees AA affiliate in Norwich, Connecticut. I had improved, advanced, and been getting paid for years, albeit not much.

During one July home stand at Dodd Stadium in Norwich, Connecticut I walked into the visiting clubhouse. It was about 3:00 pm, and the visiting Harrisburg Senators had just arrived to the ballpark. As the players unpacked their bags into their lockers, I entered the visiting manager's office. Doug Sisson looked up and gave me a big smile. We shook hands and had a great talk, reminiscing about that great season in 1994. It was great to see a baseball friend after six years, and never forgot how he made me feel like part of the team years earlier.

-Rick Schultz

Out Cold

On May 26, 1995, during the second game of a (seven-inning) doubleheader, the fifth inning, former Utah Jazz coach and team president Frank Layden sings "Take Me Out to the Ballgame", and when he finishes, I sat back down in my seat, pull up the chair, and I bang my knee on the counter. I was in midsentence and I passed out on the air. My wife was in the seat next to me and on the tape I heard her later saying, 'Steve? Steve?'

Albuquerque at the time was traveling two guys and they didn't like each other so one would leave when the other was on the air, and the one guy always liked to hang around the other team's booth. So he had just come in after I passed out, so he took my headphones off and said, "Well, Steve has got a little bit of a problem, this is Jim Lawwill here filling in for Steve." I slowly but surely kind of came to. The team doctor was here and he took me into the owner's suite to recuperate on the couch.

While they were trying to figure out what to do with me, David Locke, who worked for our flagship station and is currently the radio play-by-play guy for the Jazz, was in the ballpark, and he came up to take my place, and the Albuquerque guy wouldn't give up the microphone. They almost got into a fight, but Locke finished the game, although I did rejoin him for the post-game show.

-Steve Klauke

Rain Delay Snack

The 1997 Hudson Valley Renegades were mired in a sloppy rain delay at Jamestown's Russell Deitrick Park. As the rain fell, most of the team stood around talking near their first-base dugout.

"Look what I found," one Renegade said, as he scooped up a ten-inch brown worm.

"Ever seen anyone eat one of those?" one player asked. "I might do it for money."

"No you won't," the backup catcher interjected, "Because I will. What will you pay me?" The players began to pool some money together.

"We've got 45 bucks," one guy said.

"Done," said the catcher, as he grabbed the long, slimy worm. Holding the worm above his head, he slowly lowered it and began chomping. With grand, pronounced chewing bites, he ate the entire worm in about 15 seconds. "That may be disgusting," he said with a smile, "But now I'll eat well tonight! I promise you that!"

-Rick Schultz

The Broadcasters

Rick Schultz began broadcasting in 1993. His career has included time calling games for the Hudson Valley Renegades, Norwich Navigators, Army Basketball, Army Hockey, Scorephone and Time Warner Cable TV. For six years he was an adjunct Sports Broadcasting Professor at Marist College and the Connecticut School of Broadcasting.

In 2000 he released "A Renegade Championship Summer", which took a behind-the-scenes ride with Josh Hamilton, Jorge Cantu, Matt Diaz and the entire 1999 Hudson Valley Renegades, on their quest toward the New York-Penn League Championship. Schultz graduated from Fordham University, interned at Sports Radio 66 WFAN in New York and was mentored by the great Marty Glickman.

Rick has coached hundreds of students and aspiring broadcasters and currently offers private sessions by appointment. His online Sports Broadcasting Course is **www.Udemy.com/sportscasting** . Contact him at **Rick@MyMidHudsonAgent.com** or follow him on Twitter **@RickSchultzNY**

Dan Besbris is the Director of Broadcasting and Media Relations for the Bakersfield Blaze, a Class A Advanced Affiliate of the Cincinnati Reds. Originally from Los Angeles, Dan spent his collegiate years at the University of California, Berkeley, where he earned his degree in Molecular and Cell Biology.

Curt Bloom is the Director of Broadcasting for the Southern League's Birmingham Barons, the Double-A Affiliate of the Chicago White Sox. He is a two-time Southern League Broadcaster of the Year, and spent a decade calling games for the UAB Blazers.

Ed Cohen served as the voice of the Billings Mustangs in 2008 and 2009 -- he called games for the Burlington Royals of the Appalachian League in 2007. In addition to his baseball work, Cohen currently is the voice of the Rutgers women's basketball team and the Manhattan College men's basketball team, in addition to his role as an update anchor for Sirius XM Sports. Cohen has also announced games on MSG Network, SNY and NBA TV -- he even covered a triathlon in Bermuda that aired on Versus, but has no immediate plans to train for a race anytime soon. During his high school years, Ed and his family toured the country visiting every Major League ballpark, while documenting the journey for a local radio station.

Phil Elson is in his 12th season behind the mic for the Arkansas Travelers, the Double-A Affiliate of the Los Angeles Angels. He joined the club in 2001 as the first full time broadcaster in Travs history. Besides being responsible for all media relations, stats and broadcasting, Phil maintains the Travs' new website, is available as a speaker for civic groups and serves as an account executive. He has 17 seasons of experience in professional baseball, including 14 years on the radio. Phil has also worked for baseball teams in Stockton, CA; Ogden, UT; Helena, MT; Akron, OH; Pittsburgh, PA and Fayetteville, NC. He was voted the 2009 Arkansas Sportscaster of the Year by the National Sportscasters and Sportswriters Association. Elson also calls radio play-by-play for the University of Arkansas at Little Rock Trojans women's and men's basketball teams along with Henderson State University football and is a professional voice-over actor. Phil was born and raised in Pittsburgh and counts the Pirates, Steelers, Penguins and Pitt Panthers as his teams. Phil and his wife Julie met at Ray Winder Field on the last day of the 2001 season.

Greg Giombarrese is the Media and Public Relations Manager for the Lakewood Blueclaws, a Class-A Affiliate of the Philadelphia Phillies. Greg returns for his third consecutive, and fourth overall, year behind the BlueClaws microphone. A 2006 graduate of Fordham University, he began his broadcasting career at WFUV, broadcasting Fordham baseball, basketball, and football games. He has also worked for USOpen.org Radio, the ESPN trivia show "Stump the Schwab," and ABC Sports Radio. An avid Yankees and horse racing fan, Greg is also a professional miniature golfer.

Jesse Goldberg-Strassler is in his fourth season as the Voice of the Lansing Lugnuts, a Class-A Affiliate of the Toronto Blue Jays. A native of Greenbelt, MD, Jesse graduated from Ithaca (NY) College in 2004. After an internship covering the Baltimore Orioles for Radio 11 WBAL, he interned with the independent Brockton Rox in 2005, hosting the pregame/postgame show for current Houston Astros broadcaster Dave Raymond. Jesse spent the 2006-2007 seasons as the #2 broadcaster for the back-to-back Southern League Champion Montgomery Biscuits before serving as lead broadcaster of the 2008 Frontier League Champion Windy City ThunderBolts, where he was honored as a Runner-Up for BALLPARK DIGEST'S Broadcaster of the Year.

Doug Greenwald is the by-play announcer for the Giants' AAA team, the Fresno Grizzlies. His first game announcing for the major league Giants was on September 6, 2009. He subsequently filled in during a July, 2010 series. His career began in 1996 with the Bend (Oregon) Bandits of the independent Western Baseball League. Greenwald also spent time with Class-A Stockton and Modesto in the California League, two years at Double-A Shreveport and one winter in Hawaii with the West Oahu CaneFires.

Tim Hagerty is currently the broadcaster for the Tucson Padres (San Diego Padres Triple-A affiliate). Before Tucson, Tim was a radio broadcaster for the Triple-A Portland Beavers from 2007-2010 and the broadcaster for the Double-A Mobile BayBears (San Diego Padres affiliate) from 2005-2007. He began his professional baseball broadcasting career with the Idaho Falls Chukars (Kansas City Royals affiliate) in 2004. While with the Royals affiliate, Hagerty made his Major League broadcasting debut, joining Kansas City's radio broadcast for a game in September against Tampa Bay. You can visit his website at www.timhagerty.com

Morgan Hawk is a native of Bloomfield, Iowa has been the radio play-by-play broadcaster of the Cedar Rapids Kernels (Midwest League, Los Angeles Angels of Anaheim) since 2011 on KMRY radio. He spent 2008 and 2009 as a radio broadcasting intern with the Kernels. Hawk graduated from the University of Iowa in 2009. He is also the radio broadcaster for Cedar Rapids Xavier High School basketball and broadcasts local high school football games on KCRG-TV 9.2.

Bryan Holland currently works for the Potomac Nationals, the Class-A Advanced Affiliate of the Washington Nationals. Previously, he served as a radio broadcasting and media relations intern with the Frederick Keys (Class A Advanced, Baltimore Orioles) for their championship season in 2007. Then, Bryan was a group sales and radio broadcasting intern for Ripken Baseball's Aberdeen IronBirds (Short-Season A, Baltimore Orioles) in the 2008 campaign. A native of Elkridge, MD, Bryan graduated from Elon University (Elon, NC) in 2009, where he earned a bachelor's degree in broadcast communications and new media. Upon completion of his communications studies, Bryan pursued freelance public address announcing and voice production opportunities before holding the position of Corporate Sales Executive and Radio Voice of the Outer Banks Daredevils (summer collegiate Coastal Plain League) for the 2010 season. Bryan was then privileged to work for the Hagerstown Suns (Class A, Washington Nationals) for the remainder of 2010 and into the 2011 slate as Director of Media Relations and Play-by-play Broadcasting, while selling corporate sponsorships, group hospitality, and season tickets. During his stay with the Suns, Bryan broadcasted and coordinated the media for two former MLB number one overall draft picks, Bryce Harper (2010) and Stephen Strasburg (2009), while handling Washington Nationals standouts, Ivan Rodriguez, Ryan Zimmerman, and Chien-Ming Wang.

Steve Klauke is the only "voice" in the Salt Lake Bees' seventeen year franchise history. He has been at the mic for 2,481 of the team's 2,490 regular season and post-season games dating back to Salt Lake's first game on April 9, 1994 when the Buzz played in Vancouver. Besides the Bees, Klauke worked on two regular season games for the Toronto Blue Jays in 2004 and two spring training games for the Angels in 2009. He has also filled in as play-by-play broadcaster for Weber State football and basketball, University of Utah basketball, Utah Jazz basketball, New Orleans Hornets basketball and Utah Grizzlies hockey. He was also the play-by-play voice for the Utah Flash of the NBA Development League its first two seasons.

Mark Leinweaver is the author of "Minor Moments, Major Memories", a book featuring 100 Major League players, coaches and managers, chronicling their most fond recollections of the Minor Leagues. From 1997-2002, he was the Director of Media Relations and Broadcasting for the Norwich Navigators, the Double-A Affiliate of the New York Yankees. Leinweaver previously broadcast for the Pittsfield Mets, the Class-A Short Season Affiliate of the New York Mets. He graduated from Stonehill College in 1997. His wide-ranging career has blossomed and he is currently a partner in a successful, up-and-coming Hollywood production company.

Jeff Levering is in his third season as the Voice of the Springfield Cardinals, the Double-A Affiliate of the Springfield Cardinals. Prior to Springfield, Jeff spent three years as the Director of Broadcasting and Media Relations with the Rancho Cucamonga Quakes. He was also with Fox Sports West/Prime Ticket in Los Angeles as a Reporter, Associate Producer, and Production Assistant. Jeff received his degree in Broadcast Journalism from Chapman University in Orange, California and was the starting Designated Hitter on the 2003 D-III National Championship baseball team.

Dave Lezotte has been the Director of Broadcasting and Media Relations and the radio play-by-play broadcaster for the Clinton LumberKings since 2006. While with Clinton, a Class-A Affiliate of the Seattle Mariners, he's had the privilege of calling three trips to the Midwest League Playoffs (including the MWL Championship Series in 2010) and the 2009 Midwest League All-Star Game. A 2005 graduate of the University of Wisconsin-Oshkosh, Dave has also worked for the Milwaukee Brewers in ticket sales and has interned with the Brewers' television broadcast team. His first-ever baseball job was as a member of the Brewers' Grounds Crew starting in 2000.

Connell McShane is a highly regarded news anchor and reporter for the Fox News Network and Fox Business Network. He also anchors news for the "Imus In The Morning" radio program. His professional baseball experience includes time as the Voice of the Pittsfield Mets, a Class-A Affiliate of the New York Mets. McShane began is broadcast journalism career at Fordham University and WFUV Radio in New York City.

Robert Portnoy has been the Albuquerque Isotopes Director of Broadcasting and play-by-play voice since coming to Albuquerque in 2006. During his tenure with the Isotopes, Portnoy has worked a number of national events, including the 2011 Triple-A Baseball National Championship, for which he was the play-by-play broadcaster for the national telecast on NBC Sports Network. Portnoy also served as the lead radio play-by-play voice of the 2007 Triple-A All-Star Game, which was broadcast nationally on the Westwood One Radio Network. Portnoy has 14 years of professional baseball broadcasting experience. In 2008, he received an Excellence in Broadcasting Award for sports play-by-play from the New Mexico Broadcasters Association. Portnoy was the basketball play-by-play voice for the NBA D-League Albuquerque Thunderbirds and is currently a show host and play-by-play broadcaster for football and basketball on ProView Networks in Albuquerque. He and his wife Tami have two children, Dana and Alyssa.

Brett Quintyne is currently working with SiriusXM in New York City. His extensive broadcasting career has included stints with Sportce Inc., Lexy and MLB.com. Quintyne spent two seasons as the Director of Broadcasting and Media Relations for the Norwich Navigators, and three seasons holding that same position for the Amarillo Dillas. Brett is a graduate of Syracuse University.

Danny Reed is the Director of Broadcasting/Play-by-Play announcer for The Citadel Sports Network. He spent four seasons as the play-by-play announcer for the Charleston Riverdogs, a Class-A Affiliate of the New York Yankees. He served as pre-game/post-game show host and occasional play-by-play fill-in during the 2008 campaign before stepping in as the interim "Voice of the RiverDogs" in August of that year. In October 2008, the interim tag was lifted and Reed was brought onto the staff full-time as the team's radio sales manager in addition to serving as the day-to-day media relations contact in the off-season.

A native of Cumberland, Md., Reed graduated summa cum laude from Waynesburg University (Pa.) with a B.A. in Communication in May 2007. He served as the primary play-by-play voice for Waynesburg men's and women's basketball and baseball and was also the voice of Greene County High School football for WCYJ-FM 88.7 (since changed to 99.5). He has worked for 1270 AM WCBC radio on a seasonal basis since November 2001 in his hometown as a play-by-play broadcaster, analyst, and statistician. Prior to coming to Charleston, Reed completed an internship with the Hagerstown Suns of the South Atlantic League's Northern Division in 2007.

Mike Saeger has been broadcasting minor league baseball play-by-play since 1991. He's had stops in Augusta, GA, Vero Beach, FL, San Bernardino, CA, and is currently the voice of the San Antonio Missions in the Texas League. In addition, Saeger has done college and high school football and college basketball. He graduated in 1990 from California State University Northridge with a degree in Broadcast Journalism. Saeger and his wife, J'Leen have one daughter (Ashlyn) and currently reside in San Antonio.

Justin Sheinis, a native of South Florida, spent one season broadcasting for the Connecticut Tigers after working for one season with the Buffalo Bisons, the Triple-A affiliate of the New York Mets. Along with writing feature stories, game recaps and producing video content for the team site, he also broadcasted over 80 games during the season for the Bisons. Born and raised in South Florida, Sheinis graduated from the University of Miami with a Bachelor of Arts in broadcast journalism. While at Miami , Sheinis worked for WVUM- FM as well as UMTV. His broadcast experience includes UM baseball, basketball, football and volleyball. He had the opportunity to travel to Omaha, NE to cover the Canes' 2008 College World Series appearance and has also covered ACC men's and women's basketball tournaments. He also spent a brief stint as a media relations assistant with the Florida Marlins. Sheinis joined the Tigers after spending the winter as the Media Relations Director and Broadcaster for the Texas Legends during their inaugural season in the NBA Development League.

Larry Ward has been broadcasting for 42 years and is a 31 year veteran of minor league baseball play by play. The 2012 season marks Larry's 24th with the Chattanooga Lookouts, a Double-A Affiliate of the Los Angeles Dodgers. Since 1989, "The Voice" has been telling the story of Lookouts baseball to thousands of loyal listeners in the Tennessee Valley. Larry also serves as the Lookouts' travel secretary and is the direct link between the Dodgers and the players that spend their summer in Chattanooga. Before joining the Lookouts, Larry held the microphone for the Portland Beavers, Tucson Torros, Jacksonville Suns, and Charleston (SC) Rainbows. He has also served as the voice of Citadel University sports. During the off-season, Larry is the voice of the UTC Lady-Mocs basketball team. Larry was inducted into the Greater Chattanooga Sports Hall of Fame in 2005.

Don't miss these books by Rick Schultz on Amazon.com:

**A Renegade Championship Summer: A Broadcaster's View of a
Magical Minor League Baseball Season**
Come along for the ride with the 1999 New York-Penn League
Champion Hudson Valley Renegades. Hear from the players and
coaches who made it happen, including superstar Josh Hamilton and
many other household names!

**101 Things I Wish I Knew Before I Bought My First Home: How
to Reduce the Stress of Your First Purchase**
Buying your first home is sure to be one of the most exciting, yet
stressful times in your life. This book will fill you in
BEFOREHAND about some of the many issues you may encounter
when you buy your home. Reduce the stress and enjoy this special
time in your life!

Rick Schultz is the Sports Director at WFUV
Radio, Fordham University. For decades, WFUV in
New York City has provided the training and
preparation for countless nationally-acclaimed
sports broadcasters and media professionals.

Contact him at:
SportscastersClub.com

Special Offer for Sports Fans:
Receive 50% off our Online Sports Broadcasting
Course
For sports fans and aspiring sportscasters
Visit Udemy.com/sportscasting
Enter promo code: JUST10

Thank you for reading.

I hope you enjoyed these
Untold Tales From The Bush Leagues!

See you at the ballpark!

Made in the USA
Coppell, TX
14 April 2020

20011732R00088